Dancing from Darkness

A WWII Survivor's Journey to Light, Life, and Redemption

By Eleanor Isaacson and Jeanette Windle

Copyright © 2017 by Eleanor Isaacson and Jeanette Windle

Eleanor Isaacson Publications

https://www.eleanorisaacson.com

ISBN 978-0-9991374-0-6 (print book)

ISBN 978-0-9991374-1-3 (e-book)

book and e-book designed and formatted by
ebooklistingservices.com

1 3 5 7 9 10 8 6 4 2
Printed in the United States of America

Dedication

I dedicate this book to my dear husband, **Robert B. Isaacson**, who not only encouraged me to get up and speak about my war-time experiences in Germany, but also encouraged me to write this book. Bob, I'm sorry you are not here with me to hold the finished copy. Thank you for eighteen wonderful years of marriage and for making all the darkness become light because of your love, devotion, and understanding. You helped me become the woman I am today.

See you in Glory.

Love 'ya,

Your Sweets

Table of Contents

Foreword

As a college president I have the privilege and opportunity to meet a lot of people in some very interesting settings. As I meet each one I always try to remember that these are not merely acquaintances to be greeted, connections to be made, but each encounter is a unique individual with a story, a story God is writing whether or not it's realized in the moment.

That said, I can tell you that when I met Eleanor Isaacson in the setting of a beautiful resort introducing people to the mission and vision of Lancaster Bible College, I was not prepared for the recounting of her remarkable journey.

We have heard much of what we have come to know as *The Greatest Generation*. My father was part of that fraternity of men who served a cause far greater than themselves during World War II, what many have termed the greatest of battles against evil and depravity. He then went on to serve Christ as a pastor for more than 60 years, fighting those battles on behalf of others differently, spiritually. However, I had yet to personally meet anyone who lived through the reality of that season embedded in Germany, much less someone who knew the pangs of abandonment, fear and an amorphous presence that seemed to be reaching out to her from her earliest years, all amidst the backdrop of Germany and a raging war. Only later in her life would she learn the name of that Presence.

Eleanor's tale is one of chaos transformed into a beautiful piece of art. It has been said that there are two views of a finely crafted tapestry—the side of its presentation where the hues and weaves create a remarkable visual expression of textile design, then the reverse side where the frays and knots are evident. Beauty from apparent chaos. I can think of no better way to describe my friend's journey.

I remain both convicted and challenged by the sweetness and depth of her soul.

—Peter W. Teague, EdD
President, Lancaster Bible College

Dancing from Darkness

Introduction

Finished Portrait

The Lord has anointed me to . . . provide for those who grieve in Zion—to bestow on them a crown of beauty instead of ashes . . .a garment of praise instead of a spirit of despair.

—Isaiah 61:1b-3a

My mother gave me away. That single puzzle piece shaped so many other pieces to follow. Enduring the oppression, bombings, and starvation of WWII Germany. Surviving Hitler only to be swallowed up into Russian-occupied East Germany. The dangers and thrills of being a preteen cross-border smuggler. Reclaiming my birth citizenship in the land of the free—America—only to discover that loneliness, rejection, and despair have no geographical boundaries.

So many gray and black and dirty-brown puzzle pieces. The sandy-beige of deafness that isolated me for so long from the colorful, noisy, interconnected world where others lived. The somber-slate of despair that anyone could love such an unloved, and therefore surely unlovable, child as I appeared to be. The ice-blue of personal loss so deep as to freeze even the well-springs of my tears.

Still, not all puzzle pieces of my life were bleak of hue, though it took me long to recognize this. There was the cheery-green of learning from nature's beauty the character of an almighty and loving Designer. The pure-white of my invisible Friend, whose presence and protection I cherished long before I knew His name. The daffodil-yellow of acquiring a family, not of my DNA, but of the heart. The spring-pink of discovering the true beauty with which my Creator had personally crafted me. The passionate flame-red of becoming one in marriage with my soul-mate and best friend.

And the most sun-bright puzzle piece of all—the day I was introduced to the Person who would heal my hurts, transform my life, and transfigure every grain of ash accumulated along my journey into a crown of beauty. Jesus Christ. Son of Man. Son of God. Redeemer of my soul.

In time, the bright colors came to outshine the dark and dreary. And if the shape, size, and color of the pieces that make up my life have in themselves been a puzzle to me, I've come to recognize that my Creator has His own purpose for every one of those pieces, the dark and the bright. In fact, I've learned that life is much like a puzzle. We choose a puzzle for the picture on the box cover. A magnificent mountain vista, perhaps. A pastural flower-dotted meadow. Or the power of a wave-tossed seascape.

But when we open the box, it is to find thousands of random fragments colored blue, green, yellow, gray, brown, black. Like our lives, it is hard to see how any single piece fits into a cohesive pattern, much less one of beauty. We look at a day that is a depressing gray or a dull brown and wonder what purpose it could hold, not knowing that in the pattern of our life it is the underside of a billowing, white cloud or the branch of a majestic, towering redwood tree.

Unlike buying a puzzle box, we cannot see from where we walk on this life's journey what our final picture will look like or even what it is intended to be. But God, who created us and knew every moment of our lives before we took our first breath, not only sees the finished image, but He has designed it to be one of beauty. In faith, we can echo the exultant prayer of King David, sweet psalmist of Israel:

> For you created my inmost being; you knit me together in my mother's womb. I praise you because I am fearfully and wonderfully made . . . My frame was not hidden from you when I was made in the secret place, when I was woven together in the depths of the earth. Your eyes saw my unformed body; all the days ordained for me were written in your book before one of them came to be.
>
> —Psalm 139:13-16

As I write this book, it is more than sixty years since I met Jesus Christ and surrendered my life to His direction. The puzzle pieces that make up each individual day are many. I don't know how many more remain before God fits the final piece into its place and at His side I will finally be permitted to see in its entirety the beautiful picture He has been crafting all these years.

But I can look back now on all I experienced of childhood neglect, war, hunger, grief, pain, loss, and I can see now that it was those very experiences God used to show me how empty is a life without Him. God used the darkest hues of my past to draw me to His light. Perhaps in my stubborn, independent nature, I would never have turned to my heavenly Father without the impetus of pain and grief. My Creator knows, and I trust His purpose in every experience, dark or bright, He has permitted me to go through.

Similarly, my dearest reader, God has a pattern and purpose for every puzzle piece that makes up your own life. Maybe right now you are living a life that seems far more hued with dingy colors than bright. Maybe the jumble of puzzle pieces that make up your days seems far more a chaotic mess than a beautiful pattern.

If so, may I encourage you to take a walk with me along my own life journey. As you read the following pages, my prayer is that you will come to see your life as I have come to see mine—an exquisite portrait designed by the Creator of Life Himself. And in that recognition, may you come to know, as I have, how deeply and eternally your Creator loves you.

Now let me invite you to step back with me to a time and place that thankfully no longer exist—the dying throes of Hitler's Third Reich.

CHAPTER ONE

AN UNMERRY CHRISTMAS

You will not fear the terror of night. . . For he will command his angels concerning you to guard you in all your ways.

—Psalm 91:5b, 11a

Could any Christmas be worse than this? Certainly not in my ten-year-old recollection! By December, 1944, Hitler's war of aggression had dragged on for more than five years. Even in such a Nazi stronghold as Plauen, a proud industrial city in central Germany near the borders of Bavaria and Czechoslovakia, residents could no longer convince themselves that their Fuehrer's powerful Wehrmacht was winning the war. Not with Allied bombs pounding Plauen to rubble for months now.

Christmas for children in Germany had always been a season imbued with glittering magic. Soft white snow cloaking Plauen's surrounding hilltops. Evergreens and other decorations lighting up the central market. Bells and carolers filling the air with music. The scents of cinnamon, molasses, ginger, anise, and chocolate from Christmas baking. The buttery flakiness of *Plätzchen* cookies and *Stollen* fruit bread melting on the tongue.

But by the final months of WWII, I'd almost forgotten the taste of such luxuries as butter, sugar, molasses. Lisbeth, as I called my aunt, guardian, and surrogate mother, had already set up a *Jul* tree in the kitchen/living-room portion of our tiny apartment. This, of course, like every other aspect of Christmas under Nazi rule, had been divested of any symbolism related to a Jewish Messiah. It represented instead the winter solstice and annual rebirth of the sun, just as the bearded man carrying a sack of gifts was no longer Saint Klaus, but the Germanic god Odin.

My dollhouse, a two-room structure of kitchen and bedroom not dissimilar to our actual apartment, had also been unpacked from storage. Like every other German girlchild, I would be allowed to play with its diminutive furnishings from Christmas Eve until the Twelfth Day of Christmas, January 6th, when it would be returned to storage until the following year. Despite food shortages, my aunt had even managed to fill its tiny food bins with the traditional real sugar and flour for me to play with. As she did every year, Lisbeth's seamstress friend Elsa had made a new dress for my doll Helga that I would unwrap with a few scant other presents on Christmas morning.

But I had no interest in doll clothes or dollhouse nor the chocolate SS soldiers, toy tanks, and fighter planes available in the town's holiday bazaar. How could this be Christmas when the very air was so permeated with fear and uncertainty I could hardly breathe? When the sound of carols, also with new lyrics that glorified Germany's great savior instead of a dead Jew, had long been drowned out by air raid sirens and bomb blasts?

As I finally fell asleep that Christmas Eve of 1944, my thoughts were not of presents. My ten-year-old existence had been reduced to a single focus—listen for the sirens, be ready always to run, hide, survive. As on every other night for months, I slept fully dressed, my shoes set neatly beside the bed so that even in the dark I could jump into them at a moment's notice.

It was 2 a.m. on Christmas morning when the air raid sirens sounded. I reluctantly pushed back my thick down comforter to face the icy night. Perhaps this time the raid would be short enough that warmth would still linger in my bed until my return. My ears hurt from the siren blare as I fumbled for my shoes. By the time I reached the door, Lisbeth had caught me by the hand. We clattered down three floors of stairs, jostling other building residents also scrambling to safety.

Our apartment building stood well up the slope of a natural basin in which Plauen sat. A cobblestone street ran downhill to the basin floor. There in the very center of the city rose a large, tree-cloaked hill. Whether by nature or with man's help, the hill had been hollowed on opposite sides into two huge caverns. In past centuries, the cold, damp interior of the caverns had provided rudimentary refrigeration for area breweries to store beer. Since the bombings began, they had been converted into air raid shelters. Some who no longer had homes to return to simply stayed there between raids.

Lisbeth and I had taken refuge in the nearest cavern many times in recent months since the bombing runs had increased from occasional to incessant. Under normal conditions, the hill was a twenty-minute brisk walk from our apartment. Slipping and sliding precariously down the slick, icy cobblestones, we reached the base of the hill in no more than ten minutes. Overhead, the thunder and lightning of exploding bombs added a staccato to the rising and falling whine of the air raid sirens.

As we ran, my glance was drawn upward. The fireworks of exploding ordnance gave the illusion of a star-strewn night sky. But surely I must be hallucinating, because it seemed that I could see beautiful Christmas trees of pure, golden light falling from the sky to dot the landscape. I tugged Lisbeth's hand. "Look, they're celebrating Christmas!"

Gripping my hand tighter, my aunt tugged me after her. "We can't stop to look! We have to keep running!"

Decades later, I shared this memory at a speaking engagement in North Carolina. After the event, a WWII veteran approached to reassure me: "You weren't hallucinating. Unlike our American bomb runs, the British had to be careful not to waste ordnance. So they would light up the ground with bright floodlights to check the drop zone before dropping their bombs. From the ground, those floodlights would look like an inverted-V of bright light."

At the time, I'd lost interest in any beauty the night sky held. We'd now reached the massive double doors that led into the nearest cavern, called *Mauerkeller*. The entrance to the other cavern, called *Hummerkeller*, was another fifteen-minute walk on the far side of the hill. All around us, other residents of our apartment building were pouring through the doors, as we'd done on every other air raid. But something in my stomach, in the fear squeezing air from my lungs, was screaming to me that we could not enter. Something terrible would happen if we did. Though there were no words, it was as clear as though a voice was giving me orders.

I yanked at Lisbeth's hand, pulling us both to a stop. "No, we can't go in there! Not tonight! Please, please, you have to listen to me! We need to run to the other cave! Please, please!"

While my urgency was undeniable, to this day I do not understand why my aunt did not just grab me with her far greater strength and force me through the doors of *Mauerkeller*. Providence, certainly. But Lisbeth was not a woman who believed in providence, nor anything that was not practical and rational. Still, that night she listened. Clutching her hand, it was now I who tugged her onward. We reached the entrance of *Hummerkeller* in what must have been an Olympic sprint. Even so, its huge doors, mirror image to those of *Mauerkeller*, were already swinging ponderously shut.

"Hold the doors!" my aunt called sharply. "We're coming!"

We nipped through the narrow opening, the doors slamming shut on our very heels. We were barely inside when the ground began shaking. The bombs had to be falling very close by. The cavern was so packed with humanity that if someone in that crowd collapsed from a heart attack, there wouldn't be room to fall to the ground. Scattered flashlights revealed terrified faces, and the screams that rose above the explosions and sirens came from male throats as well as women and children.

I threaded my way to the cavern wall, where I found a stone protrusion just high and wide enough to use as a chair. The rock at my back was cold and clammy, but the body heat from so many people offered enough warmth I began to feel drowsy. Relaxing into my perch, I talked to myself, since it was far too noisy to talk to anyone else. Or maybe the invisible Friend, the Presence whose identity I did not know, but who had become so real to me, was really the person I spoke to.

What is death? Am I going to die before this war is over? If I get hit by a bomb, where do I go? What happens afterward? Why must we live like this with so much fighting and death? Is there any place in this world I can go to find safety? Why am I even alive? Why am I here in the Hummerkeller? Whose voice did I hear that told me to run here?

My questions shifted to that invisible, yet so real Presence. *Who are you? What are you? Where are you?* Then, *how can I know you?*

At last, the ground stopped shaking and the all-clear siren blared. Wearily, I climbed down from my perch and made my way with Lisbeth back out the doors of the cave. The rest of the people scattered back towards their homes, since they came from that side of the city. But Lisbeth and I had to make our way back around the base of the hill to the *Mauerkeller* entrance, from which the cobblestone street would take us back up the steep slope to our apartment.

When we reached the far side of the hill, I was stunned at what I saw. The tall double-doors leading into *Mauerkeller* were not standing open so that those who'd found shelter there could exit. Instead, the entire hillside was one huge pile of rubble. The entrance had evidently received a direct hit, blowing in the doors and collapsing the entire cavern. We would learn later that hundreds of people had been crushed or smothered to death.

I could not believe what I saw. If I had not listened to that wordless internal voice, Lisbeth and I would be among the dead. But why were we alive and not these others? Who had told me to flee?

Lisbeth looked as stunned as I felt. Then she took my hand and led me away. As we started up the steep street to our home, she shook her head matter-of-factly. "Well, Eleanor, I guess God didn't want us to die tonight."

Her words were as dumbfounding as our narrow escape. Lisbeth and all her family were atheists, as Hitler had directed all good German citizens to be. In my ten years of life, I'd never been to church. I'd never seen a Bible. I'd never heard of Jesus, met a Christian, or heard anyone pray. I had no memory of anyone mentioning God before. And yet, perhaps someone at some time had, because I understood the dictionary definition of my aunt's words.

That moment was a revelation that changed my life forever. I'd long sensed there was something bigger than me in this world. Not just something, but Someone greater than all this. And now it was clear that this Someone knew *me*, Eleanor. Not just knew, but cared enough to intervene personally in my life.

As we trudged away from that silent tomb of rock and flesh, I did not ask Lisbeth what she meant by her words. But I again turned my silent queries heavenward. *Is that who my invisible Friend is—God? If it is, then how did you tell me not to go to the Mauerkeller, where we've been going since October, with no voice, no papers falling from the sky with instructions, nothing? I wish I could know you like you know me. Then maybe I wouldn't have to be so afraid to die. I wouldn't have to run anymore because you always know*

*where I am, and if I knew you as you know me, then you
would keep me safe.*

Many years later and thousands of miles from Plauen,
when I finally held in my hands a Bible, I came across in its
pages words that could have been God's direct answer to my
cry:

> He who dwells in the shelter of the Most High will
> rest in the shadow of the Almighty. I will say of the
> LORD, "He is my refuge and my fortress, my God, in
> whom I trust . . . He will cover you with his feathers,
> and under his wings you will find refuge . . . You will
> not fear the terror of night, nor the arrow that flies
> by day . . . For he will command his angels
> concerning you to guard you in all your ways; they
> will lift you up in their hands, so that you will not
> strike your foot against a stone.
>
> —Psalm 91, selected verses

That night I knew only that I was alive. And that Someone
had saved me. In the paling dawn light of that cheerless
Christmas morning, the stench of explosives and dust and
burnt flesh stinging my nostrils, I vowed from the very depth
of my lonely, love-starved, ten-year-old heart, *I know you are
real. And I know that you had a purpose in sparing my life. If
you let me live through this war and grow up to be a woman,
I am going to seek for this purpose. And I am going to find you
as a friend.*

I kept that vow.

Or rather, God did.

CHAPTER TWO

ABANDONED

Can a mother forget the baby at her breast and have no compassion on the child she has borne?

—Isaiah 49:15

I was born in the United States, and as much as my mother's abandonment would define my life journey, so would reclaiming my birth citizenship. Though I had no memory of being an American or of life with my parents as a child.

Both my paternal grandparents, Otto and Minna Drechsler, and maternal, Paul and Elsa Handel, were from Plauen. In their youth, the city was at its peak as an industrial boomtown, most famous for mechanizing the production of fine lace. *Opa* (grandpa) Otto was a baker by trade. Conscripted into the Germany army during WWI, he had the misfortune of being captured by the Russians and sent to a labor camp. Once his captors tasted his breads and pastries, they were so impressed that he was allowed to serve his sentence in the camp bakery.

When he returned home after the war, Otto decided to open a bakery of his own. Now married, he raised three sons to work with him in the bakery. By this time, Minna's sister, Tante [aunt] Klara and her husband Mike had immigrated to the United States, where they had started a bakery in Newark, New Jersey. The couple had no sons of their own. So in 1927, they invited my father, Arthur, and his two brothers Kurt and Eric, to come over and work in the bakery.

Arthur was eighteen years old at the time. He and my mother, Hilda, had been grammar school sweethearts, and he agreed to immigrate only if Tante Klara sponsored Hilda to come over as well. She agreed, and once my mother joined my father in New Jersey, they were married. While Arthur worked in the bakery, Hilda found a job cleaning houses.

But marriage quickly proved a disappointment to the childhood sweethearts. Both struggled with learning English and adapting to American culture. They also quickly demonstrated their emotional immaturity. Only eighteen when they married, Hilda was a very pretty girl who liked parties and expected always to be the center of attention. She resented the menial labor of cleaning other people's houses as much as my father resented the lower-class status of a day laborer in someone's else's bakery. Also attractive to the opposite sex, Arthur was athletic and considered himself to be quite a sportsman, especially as a soccer player. This gave him opportunities to meet other women. Hilda eventually found out about his affairs, which increased the strain on their marriage.

My parents had been married seven years when Hilda discovered she was pregnant. Like most immigrants starting out, Arthur and Hilda had little money. Still, unlike many others, they had family nearby and two steady incomes. They had no other children to support, while countless other immigrant families were working hard to feed and clothe growing families. So to this day it is hard for me to understand what followed.

When as a teenager, I met Hilda for what was to me the first time, she informed me almost immediately that when the doctor gave her the news that she was carrying me in her womb, her first action was to go home and begin moving the refrigerator around, hoping the exertion would bring on a miscarriage. When that didn't work, she angrily resigned herself to the pregnancy. On November 7, 1934, at the age of twenty-five, she gave birth to a daughter, Eleanor Drechsler.

If Hilda furiously resented the responsibility of raising a child, Arthur was angry that I was not born a son, instead of a daughter. Or so my mother also told me in time. I have no memory of either parent. But from other details she eventually regaled me with, Hilda alternated between ignoring me completely and dressing me up like some collectible doll. From the few photos I have of my infancy, I was indeed a pretty baby with luxurious black curls and big, long-lashed eyes. Hilda would put rouge on my cheeks and tint my lips to show off to her friends.

If either Hilda or Arthur hoped having a child would bring them closer together, it was an abysmal failure. According to my mother, my father was jealous of any attention she gave me. Certainly nothing that happened in later years would indicate Arthur had any more interest in his baby daughter than Hilda. All of which culminated in my mother deciding to give me away. Her rationale, as eventually explained to me, was that her shaky relationship with her husband might improve without a two-year-old running around. If this was indeed her hope, it again proved an abysmal failure.

Regardless, Hilda booked passage for herself and me on a ship to Germany. Once we arrived at my maternal grandparents' home in Plauen, she began going door to door, asking if anyone wanted a little girl named Eleanor. When Oma (grandma) Elsa discovered Hilda's activities, she was furious.

"You are a terrible woman!" she reportedly screamed at Hilda. "What kind of mother gives her baby away? Get out of my house. I never want to see you again."

Hilda left the house and indeed never saw her parents again. But she remained adamant that she was returning alone to the USA, regardless of whether someone took me. What might have happened if it came to this point, I will never know. But that was when my mother's younger sister Lisbeth and her husband Walter stepped forward. While not wealthy, they owned a prosperous beauty salon, and they had now been married for several years without conceiving children of their own. They agreed to take me in. Handing over my birth certificate and other pertinent paperwork, Hilda set sail back to New Jersey.

Perhaps one of the more bizarre elements of this story is that when Hilda returned without his only child, Arthur never asked her what she'd done with me. The story Hilda told friends and family who asked was that I'd gotten sick while in Plauen, and she'd left me there so as not to disrupt my medical care. If so, she never explained why she never bothered going back to retrieve me. Especially once Hitler's invasion of Poland in September, 1939, kicked off an escalating war in the homeland where she'd abandoned her daughter. As to her relationship with my father, rather than being improved by freedom from child care, the marriage ended in divorce just a few years after I was left in Plauen.

Today I can say honestly that I have forgiven both my parents. I've even learned to thank God for giving me such parents, because their abandonment helped forge me into the woman I am today. It gave me the compassion and empathy for others Hilda and Arthur never had. I've been able to mentor and, yes, mother, so many young people who have also been neglected, rejected, and abused.

But understanding why my mother in particular could so easily discard her only child with as little apparent emotion as tossing out some unwanted package has been harder to grapple with. In time, I learned that Hilda had been born out of wedlock and had in turn been made to feel an embarrassment and inconvenience. Had her return home with me been some desperate bid for her own mother's love? How had she felt when Oma Elsa threw her out and made clear she never wanted to see her daughter again? Was Hilda's treatment of me just a repeat cycle of the lack of mothering she herself had received?

Whatever the reason makes no real difference in the end. And if I was left motherless, I came in time to know the true Parent to the motherless and fatherless. Many centuries ago, when God's own chosen people, the children of Israel, wailed that they had been forgotten and forsaken, God gave them this reminder:

Can a mother forget the baby at her breast and have no compassion on the child she has borne? Though she may forget, I will not forget you! See, I have engraved you on the palms of my hands.

—Isaiah 49:15-16a

I was sad proof that there are mothers who can indeed forget and lack compassion for the children they've borne. Which makes the image of God's love portrayed in these verses even more precious to my heart. Many parents keep a photo of their children on their desk or in their wallet. Some might even get a tattoo of their child's name. I, the motherless, the fatherless, can rejoice that my Creator, my heavenly Father, will never forget or abandon me. He loves me so much as to engrave my name in everlasting memorial on the very palms of His hands.

CHAPTER THREE

HITLER

For this is what the LORD says . . . As a mother comforts her child, so will I comfort you.

—Isaiah 66:12-13a

Of course at this time, I had no idea I'd been abandoned. My earliest memories were not unhappy. I lived with my aunt Lisbeth and my uncle Walter on a street in central Plauen called *Trochenthal Strasse*. Their beauty salon was on the first floor, while we lived in a comfortable, if small, apartment on the fifth floor. Since Lisbeth and Walter both spent most of their time working, our kitchen was also on the first floor next to the salon.

My earliest memories are of the salon. Dressed in a frilly dress with a bow in my thick black curls, I would wheel my tricycle around the salon while Walter trimmed hair and beards and Lisbeth gave perms and manicures. Or I would push my baby carriage with a doll inside. The salon patrons treated me like a princess, giving me candy and playing with me. At tea time, Lisbeth would make hot chocolate next door in the kitchen. Bringing me a cup of chocolate and half a butter roll, she would let me sit in one of the salon chairs just like an adult customer and dip my roll in the hot chocolate. Yummy!

But I wasn't too old before I began to realize that in one aspect I was different from other children I knew. They all had a mother and a father. I had Lisbeth and Walter, but though they'd taken me into their home, they never had me call them Mutter and Vater. Nor even Tante and Onkel (uncle). I never called my aunt anything but Lisbeth, and her husband was Walter.

Nor did Lisbeth and Walter treat me as their daughter, though again I did not know the difference for many years. They fed me, clothed me, and treated me kindly. But not once do I remember Lisbeth hugging and kissing me or Walter lifting me onto his lap. Both sets of my grandparents still lived in Plauen, and, in fact, *Drechsler Bakerie*, owned by *Opa* Otto, was right down the block from the salon. But I saw Otto and Minna only on those occasions when Lisbeth would take me to the bakery to purchase bread or pastries. They never mentioned my father and, to my knowledge, never inquired to find out why Arthur had sent his only daughter away.

We visited *Opa* Paul and *Oma* Elsa once a month, and I came to know some of my aunts, uncles, and cousins. But though I certainly felt wanted and even loved by my maternal relatives, I again have no memories of hugs, a kiss on the cheek, or any other physical display of affection. In Germany, especially under Nazi rule, children were not pampered, but raised to be tough and strong, future soldiers for Hitler's Reich.

Hitler had become chancellor of Germany in January, 1933, almost two years before my birth. He was not unpopular in Plauen. In fact, Plauen had been the site of the Nazi party's first chapter outside Hitler's home base of nearby Bavaria. That popularity came in part because Hitler controlled what Germans heard on the radio and read in the newspapers. All we heard in Plauen was what a wonderful leader Hitler was and how he was restoring German prosperity.

Even Hitler's aggression against surrounding nations was explained as a demonstration of his concern for the German people. The Germans were superior, smarter, and more industrious than other nationalities. They deserved more territory for their expanding population, and Hitler was driving out less worthy ethnicities to make room for Germans to prosper. This strategy was called *Lebensraum*, or "living space", and it was based on Hitler's belief that the racially superior Germans had every right to displace lesser races like the Eastern Europeans and repopulate their land with German colonies.

I would have just turned four the night of November 9-10, 1938. That night would go down in history as *Kristallnacht*, or "Crystal Night" in reference to the shattered glass that littered the streets by morning. *Kristallnacht* was a coordinated attack carried out by both SS troops and rioting civilians against Jewish businesses, synagogues, hospitals, schools, and homes all across Germany. Their justification was the assassination of a Nazi diplomat, Ernst vom Rath, at the German embassy in Paris by a Polish teenager of Jewish descent named Herschel Grynszpan. An estimated 7000 Jewish businesses and 1000 synagogues were destroyed in one night. Countless Jews were murdered or rounded up to be sent, as we would eventually learn, to concentration camps.

As such a small child, I wouldn't have been exposed to any of this. But years later, *Onkel* Warner, an uncle on my father's side who had some disability that kept him out of the army, told me how he'd seen Plauen's synagogue burning that night. He'd gathered several neighbors and headed to the police station, assuming perhaps the police hadn't yet been informed of the situation. But when he reported the fire to the officer in charge, the policeman just sat there, staring down at the papers on his desk.

"Aren't you going to do something?" *Onkel* Warner kept asking. When the police officer kept ignoring him, one of the neighbors nudged my uncle in the ribs, whispering, "I think we'd better leave."

That was when *Onkel* Warner realized the police not only knew about the situation, but were permitting it. He and his companions returned home, unhappy about the situation, but aware that if they verbalized their anger, they too would become targets of the SS. What would have happened if they and other Germans had stood their ground to help their Jewish neighbors, we will never know. That passive acquiescence certainly emboldened Hitler, who just ten months later would invade Poland, ushering in WWII.

I knew little of this at the time. But a radio played in the beauty salon for the entertainment of its clients. After the war started, we would listen to its reports of Germany's brave Wehrmacht (armed forces) fighting the British and French oppressors. We could hear the roar of fighter planes and bombers over Berlin, the staccato of anti-aircraft guns and the shrill whine of sirens. Of course, the news announcers always proclaimed that the Germans were winning these air battles. Hitler's own voice often boomed over the airwaves.

"You German people are special," he would scream. "You are the Aryan race. We will conquer the world to make it a better place. To give you more space because you are so industrious and smart."

The salon patrons and neighbors crowding around to hear the radio believed him. Why shouldn't they? The war had not yet touched Plauen. Its residents had prospered under Hitler's iron-fisted leadership. If there were negative aspects to that leadership, those were not publicized.

For me, Hitler's rants and noisy reports from the front lines were no different from any other radio theater program. Sometimes I played "war", going out into the hall and making sounds of an air raid siren. When Lisbeth and Walter hurried out with a blanket as though taking shelter from the bombs, I would inform them sternly, "It's only make-believe!"

Our region of Germany near the borders of Bavaria and Czechoslovakia was strongly Roman Catholic. But my own extended family had no religious affiliation at all. Whether this was due to Nazi pressure or a longer family heritage, I did not know then nor know now. Certainly in coming years, I personally would experience the heavy hand of the Nazi party in suppressing the worship of any deity beyond Hitler himself. I had never attended church, seen a Bible, or heard anyone pray. I had no concept of what "God" and "Jesus Christ" signified except as curse words.

But when I was four years old, one of the salon customers invited me to be the flower girl in a wedding. My aunt and uncle consented. The wedding was held in the historic

Johanniskirche (St. John's Church), a stately cream-colored cathedral with black slate roof and twin bell towers topped with onion-shaped cupolas.

I remember vividly walking down the aisle of that majestic sanctuary in my beautiful white dress, holding a basket of rose petals. As I scattered the petals ahead of the bridal party, the exquisite solemnity of the organ music brought something to life inside me. I did not even have words for it, but the atmosphere inside that church was so different from everyday life, spiritual, holy, as though for that short moment I was connected to the Divine, even though I'd never heard of God. That memory would return to me in future years.

CHAPTER FOUR

LATCH-KEY CHILD

When my father and my mother forsake me, then
the Lord will take me up.

—Psalm 27:10, KJV

The somewhat idyllic bubble in which I lived burst
when my uncle Walter was drafted into Hitler's war
machine, along with all other able-bodied men in
Plauen. And like most of those drafted soldiers, my uncle
never did come home. What I remember most is Lisbeth's
tears. If the front lines were still hundreds of miles to the
west, the war had now become real to us. With the men gone,
industry and commerce slowly crumbled. The salon
eventually closed for lack of customers.

By that time, I had started school. Under the Nazi regime,
school was little different than a military boot camp. In fact,
Hitler saw the education system as critical to indoctrinating
the next generation in Nazi philosophy. All teachers were
required to be Nazi party members and to teach a Nazi-
approved curriculum. History and biology were especially
impacted by the new curriculum. Germany's loss in WWI was
blamed on the Jews, Marxists, and other powers jealous of

German superiority. Racial instruction taught the purity and superiority of the Aryan race and the evil of mixing German blood with other inferior ethnicities. Jews especially, but also other sub-humans like the Poles, Slavs, and other Eastern Europeans.

An avid reader, I could have loved learning were it not for the trauma of school under the Nazis. Lisbeth was now supporting us as a factory worker, like so many German women whose menfolk were off fighting Hitler's war. The factory where she worked made bandages for the army and hospitals.

So at just six years old, I found myself a latch-key child. School was a half-hour walk each way. Traditionally, the first day of school was a celebratory event for German children. Their parents would meet them after the first day of class with hugs, kisses, and a meter-tall cone filled with candy called a *zuckertuete*. Children would pose for photos with their *zuckertuete*, then walk home with their parents for a celebratory supper.

At the end of my first day, Lisbeth did leave work early to come to the school and walk home with me. But she was not carrying a *zuckertuete*. I felt devastated as other children with their mothers and cones streamed past me. But Lisbeth simply explained, "Well, Eleanor, I want you to grow up to be a strong girl. You don't need everything other people have."

Maybe she is right, I thought as we walked home. After all, I was different from my classmates. They had mothers and fathers. I still had never been told why I had none. I did not even have an aunt, only a Lisbeth, as though she were my sister or not family at all.

It's okay if I'm different from other girls, I reassured myself. But when we reached our apartment, I discovered a large *zuckertuete* standing in a corner. Whether Lisbeth truly intended to teach me a lesson or simply forgot the cone, I don't know, but I was happy.

But I was not happy at school. Each day began with a salute to Hitler, represented by his picture displayed prominently on the wall. When our teacher entered the classroom, we had to jump to attention, click our heels, extend our right arm, and shout, "Heil Hitler!" Then placing the right hand over our hearts, we recited a pledge of allegiance to Hitler and the Nazi party. If a student's stance was sloppy or an arm drooped down, the teacher would take a thin rod and crack it repeatedly across the student's fingers. Crying during such punishment was forbidden.

"You are soldiers!" the teacher would harangue us. "You are German! If you are German, you do not cry!"

Even outside of school, a teacher had despotic authority. If we encountered our teacher on the street, we were expected to salute with a "Heil Hitler". If we didn't, we could expect him to walk over and slap or beat us right there on the street.

If this didn't happen to me, it was only because I was a very cowed child, quiet and submissive in class. We sat all day at our desks on hard, wooden benches. We had no paper to write on, so we used a slate board and chalk to do our school exercises. There were few books, but I do remember a Hans Christian Anderson book of fairy tales. There was also a large map tacked up on the wall, which the teacher used to show the progress of the Nazi war effort. We would eventually learn that much of this so-called progress was a lie.

Our classrooms were not heated, and as the school year advanced, the cold and snow made walking to and from school more unpleasant. Eventually, Lisbeth took one of our old blankets and had it cut into a coat for me. Even so, I was always cold. I also lived in daily fear of whether I'd be hit by the teacher. One day when I was seven, I was assigned to write in class my first composition, its topic how wonderful Hitler was. I still remember the date—February 8, 1943—because I forgot to include the comma after the day of the month. My teacher ordered me to the front of the class, then whipped me across the fingertips of both my hands.

By now, the happy, outgoing child who had been spoiled and pampered by my aunt and uncle as well as all their salon patrons was long gone. With Walter gone, Lisbeth withdrew more and more into her own unhappiness. She was not unkind to me. She worked hard to provide for my needs as well as hers. Unlike my mother, she never even considered abandoning me. Perhaps she truly loved me. After all, she had been my only mother and I her only child since I was two years old. But she worked long hours, and it was not part of her pragmatic, no-nonsense character to lavish praise or physical affection on me.

I in turn was a very sensitive, lonely child, and I took her seeming disinterest as rejection. After all, by now I understood she was not my mother, just a relative who'd been kind enough to take me in when my own parents didn't want me. More and more, I turned inward into my own mind, becoming a very imaginative, introverted child.

One other significant memory stands out from those early years. My aunt Friedel, wife of Lisbeth's brother Wilhelm, lived in the *Dopfmarkt*, the city's central market district famed for the decorative pots and fine lace sold there. Her daughter Ruth was two years younger than I. Like Lisbeth's husband Walter, my uncle Wilhelm had been conscripted into the army. With both men gone, the four of us spent a lot of time together. Since Lisbeth worked long hours, I would go to Tante Friedel's house after school, where Lisbeth would pick me up after work. On Fridays, we would stop at the butcher shop before heading home, where we would purchase an eighth-pound of baloney. The bakery was next door, and we would stop there next to purchase a fresh, warm roll with butter and jelly. That was my special treat to eat while we walked home.

On this particular evening, we were emerging from the bakery when I noticed two men across the narrow cobblestone street. They were working hard to chop ice away from the sidewalk. Though dusk was darkening quickly to night, I could see clearly the beautiful golden six-pointed star on their armbands and that both looked thin and sad.

"Why is it that everyone wearing that pretty star always look so sad, and everyone with that ugly black spider on their arm always look so angry?" I asked Lisbeth. I knew well the anger because my teacher was among those who proudly wore that black spider on his arm band.

I would eventually learn that the "spider" on its blood-red background was actually a swastika, Hitler's chosen symbol. But Lisbeth answered matter-of-factly, "I think Hitler doesn't like the people with that pretty star."

"Why?" I demanded loudly, giving the two men a puzzled stare. After all, that golden six-pointed star was much prettier than the black spider.

"Shh, Eleanor!" Lisbeth hissed, then dropped her voice to answer, "I don't know."

As she led me hurriedly down the sidewalk, I looked back at the two men. They stopped chopping ice to look back at me. For a long moment, we stared at each other, a small, curly-haired German girl-child and two Jewish slave laborers, as I eventually learned they were. Young as I was, I felt an invisible connection, some spark of shared humanity that wrenched at my heart.

Why does Hitler hate them so? I wondered. Then rebellion surged up in me. Fiercely, I vowed as I turned away from the two men, *Someday when I grow up, I am going to show that Hitler! I'm going to marry one of those people with the pretty star!*

And that is exactly what I did. One day, I would not only marry a Jewish man, but I would help him find his Messiah, Jesus Christ. Dear reader, maybe you find it hard to believe that a seven-year-old could have made such a vow. But to this day, I remember vividly that experience and the thoughts that went through my heart and mind. I was only seven years old, but in a war there is no such thing as childhood. Children enduring hardship and trauma grow up quickly, and if my body was still a child's, my mind was not!

CHAPTER FIVE

RISING TIDE

I have learned the secret of being content in any and
every situation . . . whether living in plenty or in
want.

—Philippians 4:12

While Walter's absence had drastically impacted
our financial circumstances, there was ample food
and plenty of work available. Hitler was still telling
the German people that they were winning the war. I
remember receiving a pair of ice skates for Christmas, the
old-fashioned type that fit over shoes and were tightened
with a key.

I still hated school, but at least I wasn't old enough to be
required to attend *Hitlerjugend*, a title which translates
simply to Hitler Youth. This was the Nazi version of the Boy
and Girl Scouts, and, in fact, was not dissimilar in its
organization, khaki and black uniforms, emphasis on
outdoor skills and athletics. Though the *Hitlerjugend*
uniform included a swastika on the arm band. Its activities
were also far more militaristic than the Scouts with lots of
marching and weapons training as well as Nazi

indoctrination. Hitler believed the key to a powerful Germany began with raising every child to be physically fit, strong German citizens committed to fight faithfully for the Nazi regime. So by age ten every child was required to join the *Hitlerjugend.*

Part of Hitler Youth indoctrination was that religion was for the weak and old, so rallies were often staged on Sunday mornings outside churches. To go inside meant walking through the marching, singing battalions and being marked down as a traitor by some Nazi party member. The subliminal message was not subtle. Inside was a dead savior hanging on a cross in a dead church, while outside strong, healthy, superior youth were worshipping a very much alive, powerful savior. The Nazis had in essence created an alternative fake church with its own fake god named Adolf Hitler.

While I was still young enough not to be required to attend, an older friend, Gertrude, had turned ten. She hated the *Hitlerjugend* meetings and one Sunday morning decided to go swimming instead. Within the hour, a Nazi officer came to Gertrude's home, demanding to know why she wasn't at the rally. Her mother tried to cover Gertrude's absence by saying she wasn't feeling well. The officer ordered her to produce her daughter at once, then demanded a bribe of three months' rent.

"What kind of mother are you to allow your daughter to disobey the Third Reich?" he screamed. "If you do not pay me, I will take your three other children, and you will never see them again."

Gertrude did not miss another rally. As the boys grew out of Hitler Youth, they were drafted into the army or the elite Nazi commando force, the *Schutzstaffel,* or SS. Hitler had another program for the girls, especially those whose blonde hair and blue eyes fit his ideal of a superior Aryan race. They would be placed in institutions called *Lebensborn*, their sole duties to be breeding partners for "racially worthy" SS officers with the purpose of raising up a superior new generation of Germans to replace the countless numbers dying in the war. Many were taken from their mothers at birth to be raised in special orphanages as elite Nazi soldiers.

Jewish children were, of course, not allowed in school by this point. Our teachers taught that the Jews were to blame for Germany losing the first world war while older students would whisper that any German child sitting next to a Jewish child would be permanently defiled. But those with physical or mental handicaps were barred as well. Hitler wanted only happy, healthy, intelligent German people.

Now, we knew nothing of concentration camps or gas chambers. Instead we were told that there were work camps, which provided employment, food, and shelter for certain groups who would not otherwise have such opportunities. After the war, we would learn that not only had six million Jews been put to death, but millions more Hitler considered subnormal—mentally or physical handicapped, those with other mental disorders, even depression, and of course political and religious dissidents. In total, Hitler would be responsible for the death of more than fifty million people.

By now it was becoming clear even in Plauen that the war was not going as well as Hitler's radio speeches claimed. Plauen was near Germany's eastern border with only the German-controlled territories of Czechoslovakia and western Poland separating us from the Soviet Union. A major factor keeping Plauen safe during the early years of WWII was

Hitler's non-aggression pact with Soviet head-of-state Joseph Stalin.

Then on June 22, 1941, Hitler abruptly invaded Russia, breaking the pact. One justification he gave was the large German colonies in the Ukraine, who deserved to live under benevolent German rule, not under the racially-inferior Russians. Regardless, it was a turning point of WWII. Hitler had powerful armies, but Russia had weather and vast territories in which to retreat. The deeper Hitler's army penetrated into Soviet territory, the more they found themselves at the mercy of snow storms and subzero temperatures. And now the Soviet Union had joined the Allied coalition, exposing Germany to attack on both eastern and western flanks.

The last time I saw my uncle Walter was when he discovered his army unit was being shipped to Leningrad. Lisbeth and I traveled up to his barracks to see him before they shipped out. He showed no tenderness towards us, only anger, and when we said goodbye, he neither hugged nor kissed either of us. As we headed down the road from the barracks, Lisbeth just stared straight ahead. But I looked back to see him standing in a window, waving at us. I would never forget the expression on his face because I'd never before seen my kind, jovial surrogate father look like that. It was an expression that said he knew he'd never see us again, that he was going to his death.

At 8 p.m. on a Thursday evening in October, 1942, the doorbell of our apartment chimed. When Lisbeth answered the door, a man stood there with the high, polished boots, puffed-out pants, and swastika armband of a Nazi officer.

Emotionlessly, he announced, "I'm here to inform you that your husband is dead."

Lisbeth's reaction was not one of tears, but rage. She screamed so angrily at the officer I was afraid she was going to kick him. If she had, he would likely have shot her. Once he left, she began to cry and scream. She did so all night, and many of our neighbors came upstairs, attempting to comfort her. Though still a small child, one thing came through clearly to me in the neighbors' words and my aunt's lamentations. That was how much they despised Hitler and the Nazis. But no one said so openly. No one dared speak against the government at all. If you did, you disappeared!

Not long after my uncle's death, the loss of the beauty salon forced us to move. Lisbeth and I now lived in a third-floor apartment on a street called Wald Strasse far enough from our prior home that I had to change schools. The apartment was just two rooms—a kitchen and a bedroom. None of the apartments had bathrooms or even a sink. For each floor, there was a sink in the hall, which was shared by five apartments.

There was also a single toilet. This was just a big pipe topped by a piece of wood with a hole in the center. It had no water, so the only flushing was by gravity. We brought buckets of water into our kitchen, where we had a plastic basin for washing. A chamber pot was our nighttime toilet. We saved newspapers to use as toilet paper.

Once again, I was a latch-key child. After Lisbeth left for work, I would lock the apartment and walk to school. Here too, all the teachers were Nazis, and the classroom was run like a military camp. At least the new school, called *Kemmler Schule*, was a much closer walk, just a few blocks from our apartment. But that meant little since, due to Lisbeth's long work hours, I would walk every day after school down to the city's central market district where Tante Frieda and her daughter Ruth lived. This was about an hour's walk, and school ended at 6 p.m., so it would be 7 p.m. when I arrived. I would stay there until Lisbeth picked me up after work, and we would walk another hour home.

No bombs had yet fallen in Plauen. But with Germany now at war with Russia, we often heard German bombers flying overhead on their way to the eastern front. Or we would see foreign bombers flying the opposite direction, and radio announcements would later tell us of Allied planes attacking Hanover or Berlin. Playing hopscotch outside in the street, I would count the planes as they crossed the sky above my head: 1-2-3-4-5-6. When their engines sounded labored, I knew their bellies were full of bombs. On the way back, they sounded lighter and faster.

In all this time, there had been no communication from my parents. By now, the war had been going on for several years. The United States had become part of the Allied coalition not long after Russia in December, 1941, when the Japanese bombed Pearl Harbor, so my parents must have been aware that their only child was now trapped in a war zone. To this day, I have no explanation as to why they made no effort to find out about my situation. I can say honestly that I have forgiven them, and I know without a shadow of doubt that God's hand was on my life from my first breath, including Nazi teachers, bombings, and all the rest.

Still, by this point, I'd become a very lonely, withdrawn, fearful child. I was always conscious that I was different from other children and did not fit in with those my own age. I never asked why I was here in Germany instead of in America, where I was born. I never asked why I had no mother or father, just Lisbeth, who provided for me but did not seem to really love me. I just accepted that I was different and let it go. I even embraced my difference. Maybe this meant there was a different life waiting for me out there than the other children of my class.

This all came to a head when I was invited to a birthday party by a girl named Maria. By now I was nine years old and in the fourth grade. Maria was a classmate, but I could tell just by looking at her that her life was completely different from mine. She came to school so beautifully dressed, her long braids always perfectly styled. She was also smart, always smiling, poised, and brimming over with self-confidence. So when she invited me to her birthday party, I was overjoyed.

I arrived at her house to discover it was a large, exquisitely furnished villa. Where Lisbeth and I lived in two dingy rooms, here I saw salons, a dining room, sunroom, gardens, even a swimming pool. The dishes were the finest china, and there was a tablecloth, napkins, and such food as I had never eaten. Everyone at the party was so well-dressed. I didn't know anything about Maria's family. Certainly at that point in the war, they must have been in favor with the Nazi regime to live in such luxury. All I saw was a lifestyle I'd never known existed.

It wasn't just the wealth I saw. There was a grace and elegance of life that sparked something in me. Lisbeth, and in fact all my extended family, were what today might be termed "blue-collar" workers. Not that there is anything demeaning in good, clean, hard labor. But they saw little value in education, especially for a girl, and had no interest at all in books, art, music, or other such things of culture. Lisbeth might praise me if I scrubbed the floor well, but bringing home good grades was not worth comment, and I could expect no help or encouragement with my studies. Ironically, one positive impact the Nazis did have was their emphasis on educating both boys and girls so that they might become strong, intelligent, productive contributors to German society.

Being in that birthday party made me realize there were other things in life besides eating and drinking and another way to live than just hand-to-mouth. More than just the beautiful villa was the graciousness with which Maria's mother treated me, a kindness I craved. Their home was so peaceful and quiet, their speech so cultured, not the noisy scrabble for survival of my own relatives. And somehow, Maria seemed to like me, though we were so different in social class and background.

Maria and I became good friends. In fact, we remain in contact to this day. She and her husband are both doctors in Plauen. At the time, it was a great boost to my own self-esteem that someone so beautiful and loved could think I was worthy to be her friend. She would invite me over to swim in the pool or play in her exquisitely-appointed room. Her mother always made me feel welcome. I'd always been artistic and loved books as much as I hated my Nazi classroom, and I came to realize that I felt more at home in this cultured, peaceful, gracious environment than in Lisbeth's apartment.

Why are these people so different from me? I asked myself. *How is it that there are people who live like this when I live in just two rooms?*

Right then I vowed to myself that when I grew up, I was going to live a lifestyle different from my relatives. A lifestyle of culture, art, education, and the finest things of life. And eventually that is exactly what I did. Of course, aiming for wealth is an empty goal in itself, as God has also taught me. If God blesses us, it is that we may use that blessing to help others and change the world for the better. But striving to better oneself, to learn, to broaden one's horizons, expand one's mind, and to enjoy all that God has placed in this world for his creation to enjoy is not wrong. I've learned to say with the Apostle Paul:

> I know what it is to be in need, and I know what it is to have plenty. I have learned the secret of being content in any and every situation, whether well fed or hungry, whether living in plenty or in want
> —Philippians 4:12

I also came to realize that what truly made Marie so different from me was knowing she was loved and living in a home filled with love. The knowledge you are loved bestows inner beauty and gives confidence that anything is possible. I'd never known that kind of love, and it would be decades before I encountered such love from another human being, a story I will share with you, dear reader, in due time.

But even at this point, I still clung to that sense of a Presence I'd first experienced as a four-year-old flower girl in St. John's Church, the feeling that somewhere out there was Something bigger than I. Someone. And though my father and mother might forsake me, perhaps this invisible Someone might be willing to take me up into His own loving embrace.

Chapter Six

War Comes to Plauen

When you pass through the waters, I will be with you; and when you pass through the rivers, they will not sweep over you.

—Isaiah 43:2a

September 9, 1944, was the day war came to Plauen. It was also what I call my first turning point in life. That day there was no school in the afternoon, so when I finished classes at noon, I walked down to Tante Friedel's home. My cousin Ruth and I were playing "mommy" in the courtyard of their apartment building, which was just a concrete slab with five outhouse-style toilets for residents. Ruth had a baby carriage, and since I was nine years old to her seven, I'd made her be my baby and was wheeling her around in the carriage when I heard a strange shushing sound overhead.

I'd never heard that particular whistling *shhhhh* before. But I'd been told that such a sound signaled a bomb falling. Sure enough, a moment later a thunderous explosion shattered the calm. I could tell it was not too close and came from the southern part of the city. Panicked, I yanked Ruth from the baby carriage, and together we ran towards the apartment building.

Other people were already running as well to take shelter in the basement, which had been designated as a bomb shelter for the apartment building in case of attack. The basement was a musty, damp place lined with large storage bins, one for each apartment, where residents kept their winter supply of potatoes, which they would purchase by the truckload in the fall. I must have taken my shoes off to play because I was barefoot as I tugged Ruth after me down the concrete steps.

At the bottom, I turned and looked back up the steps. People were still crowding down past me, filling up all the space between the bins. We could hear the roar of the bombers and other explosions in the distance as the door was slammed shut and barred, leaving us all in darkness. I say today that I aged fifty years at that moment. I was no longer a little girl aged nine, but a fifty-nine-year-old woman! Today in my eighties, I feel more youthful and carefree than I did in that dark, dank basement.

In my mind, I could envision the shattered buildings and broken bodies in the neighborhood where I'd heard that first explosion. What if the plane had dropped it on our courtyard instead of just a few hundred meters further south? I would be dead right now. So would Ruth and all these other people squeezed into the cellar with me.

This led me to a more profound thought. Why had the bomb landed over there and not here? That moment was when the certainty of an invisible Presence became truly real to me for the first time. I had not yet connected that Presence with God or even heard God ever mentioned. But I began piecing together, like a handful of puzzle pieces, a train of logic that led to an inescapable conclusion. *Someone arranged that bomb to fall over there instead of over here. And whoever that Someone is, he must be very smart to know where the bombs would fall. And he must know me too and like me a little to keep the bomb from killing me.*

It was at this point that I began a relationship I really did not understand at all. In fact, there were many times I wondered if it was simply imaginary. Maybe I was just talking to myself when I addressed that invisible Friend I'd become convinced was watching over me. But talk to my invisible Friend I did from that day forward, and for the first time in years, I no longer felt so alone.

We stayed in the shelter for perhaps a half hour, though each minute seemed to drag on to an eternity. When the all-clear sirens blared, and we climbed back out, it was into a different world. Before we went down into that basement, Plauen had behaved as though there was no war. Yes, many men had been drafted into the army. But we still had food, work, prosperity. We had no blackout curtains, no air raid drills, or assigned bomb shelters. Hitler had promised us we were winning the war.

Now we were all conscious that more bombs would be coming. And though no one said anything outright, there was a recognition that the war was lost. When I overheard adults talking, they never blamed the American and British bombers for our troubles, but Hitler. Perhaps the realization that Germany's glorious Wehrmacht was losing to the Allied Forces gave people courage to voice their anger against the Nazi regime.

The next day after that first bombing, Lisbeth didn't go to work. Instead, we walked over to the section of Plauen where the bombs had fallen. One of my maternal aunts named Klarla lived there. She was unharmed, but the building directly across from her apartment had been demolished, so Lisbeth and I crossed the street to look at the rubble. Tante Klarla was distraught, babbling about death and what was life all about and when would be the next attack.

But there were no more bombings immediately. Lisbeth returned to her job, I returned to school, and the city gradually returned to some semblance of normality. Still, the atmosphere had changed to one of constant fear and uncertainty. Stores emptied as people began stockpiling food. At night we kept windows blacked out so passing aircraft could not spot lights. It was at this time that we began sleeping at night in our clothes with shoes set out beside the bed so we could run out the door and take shelter any time the sirens went off.

All this made paying attention in school very difficult. Instead of listening to the teacher, we were always straining our ears for the roar of aircraft overhead. But school was no longer a priority, not even to the teachers. Life's purpose had been reduced to nothing more than surviving the next hour, the next day, the next bombing raid.

When the next raid did come, the bombs were again nowhere close-by. Most of the city was still standing, though glass from blown-out windows littered the streets much as it had on *Kristallnacht*. My maternal grandfather, *Opa* Otto, like many men too old to fight, was working at a munitions factory near the center of Plauen, making panzers, a light battle tank, for the army. Like other military-related sites, the factory would eventually be targeted specifically for demolition by Allied bombers. But at this point, there was little damage to the city center, so I continued walking down after school to Tante Friedel's apartment.

As I've shared already, dear reader, there was no childhood left in me by this time. I was nine years old, but my heart and mind were decades older. Gone was my enjoyment of books, dolls, nature. My aspirations to one day achieve an elegant, gracious life like Maria's now seemed trivial. Instead, I lived with constant questions. *What do I have to do to avoid being hit by the heavy bombs? Where do I run? What is a safe place in this world?*

There had to be more reason to go on living than just getting up each morning, going to school, coming home, going to bed, and waiting to die. Especially since I was terrified at the thought of dying. If I did get hit, where would I go? Not my body, which would be blown to bits, but the real Eleanor who lived inside my body.

Though this period was truly terrifying, today I can be glad that I went through it all, if for just one reason. Those horrible months of never knowing whether I would still be alive by the next day taught me the hard way that every day is a beautiful gift that should not be wasted. Every single day that God grants us has its purpose in his plan for our lives and is an opportunity to learn, to grow, and to serve our Redeemer.

The psalmist tells us in Psalm 90:12: "Teach us to number our days, that we may gain a heart of wisdom." I have taken those words to heart, and to this day, I try not to waste one moment of my life. That has made me ultra-organized and a multi-tasker, which may not always be good. But I become very frustrated when I hear people using the phrase "let's kill time", as though time were something to squander. Each day God gives to us is a day that will never come again. It may be our last day on this earth.

So each day, I make it my goal to do something that will make the world a better place, that will help another person. When I go to sleep each night, I review what I have accomplished. Perhaps something I have written. A child I have helped. A person I have mentored. It's like the last stanza of the famous Rudyard Kipling poem: "If you can fill the unforgiving minute full of sixty seconds worth of distance run, then yours is the world and all that's in it . . ."

And that includes bad days as well. We can be thankful that they too will never come again. But we need to look at even those days from a spiritual point of view, recognizing that God has a purpose for them. Perhaps this day's crisis is preparing you to be better equipped for an even bigger crisis down the road. If there is one thing I've learned through the good days and bad, the bright puzzle pieces and the dark ones, it is that God has never promised us a life without trials. Just look at the life of Jesus. If God permitted his own Son to go through so much suffering, who are we to think we deserve to never know pain?

On the contrary, it is the trials that God uses to take us beyond our natural selves, to mature us into godly, spiritual people. As the apostle James reminds us (James 1:2-4):

> Consider it pure joy, my brothers and sisters, whenever you face trials of many kinds, because you know that the testing of your faith produces perseverance. Let perseverance finish its work so that you may be mature and complete, not lacking anything.

What God in his immeasurable love does promise is to be with us on the days it feels we are drowning or passing through scorching fires of adversity as much as he is with us on the days when we are dancing with joy. One of my favorite promises in Scripture can be found in Isaiah 43:1-4:

> But now, this is what the Lord says—he who created you . . . Do not fear, for I have redeemed you; I have summoned you by name; you are mine. When you pass through the waters, I will be with you; and when you pass through the rivers, they will not sweep over you. When you walk through the fire, you will not be burned; the flames will not set you ablaze . . . Since you are precious and honored in my sight, and because I love you.

Though I did not yet know it in those fall months of 1944, God had chosen me. He knew my name. He had a purpose in every terrible event to make me the woman I am today, able to love, forgive, mentor, counsel people going through abuse, abandonment, crisis, loneliness. And though I could not see him and did not recognize he was there, God never abandoned me even in the worst of moments.

CHAPTER SEVEN

PRESCIENCE

He [Jesus] told this parable: a farmer went out to
sow his seed . . . This is the meaning of the parable:
The seed is the word of God . . . The seed on good
soil stands for those with a noble and good heart,
who hear the word, retain it, and by persevering
produce a crop.

— Luke 8:5a, 11, 15

In the months following that first bomb attack, the
uncertainty was almost as bad as the bombs themselves.
We lived every moment of every day braced for the roar of
bombers overhead and the whoosh of dropping bombs. But
in fact, it was almost two weeks after my epiphany in the
apartment basement before the next air raid hit. This time it
was nowhere near our part of the city.

Over the next month, the raids continued to come about
once a week. So long as the explosions weren't near us, life
took on a new semblance of normal. Students returned to
school, adults to work. Still, school had become no more
than a temporary shelter where we sat at our desks, paying

no attention to the teacher, straining our ears to the skies, until the air raid siren wailed. At which point we would hurry to our designated shelter or basement.

By mid-October, the air raids were coming more frequently, two or three times a week. We could tell the bombers apart by their markings. The Americans with their red, white, and blue flags typically dropped bombs by day. Night runs were the British with their St. George's cross. Many times, the air sirens went off in the middle of the night, but no bombs followed. By this point, Lisbeth and I, along with all others in our apartment building, were taking shelter in the caves. Between false alarms and actual bombing raids, we rarely enjoyed an undisturbed night's sleep.

The air raids supposedly focused on targets of military significance such as the ammunitions and tank factory where my grandfather worked. But there were now buildings reduced to rubble all over the city and even more blown out windows. By the time I turned ten years old on November 7th—no birthday celebration, however small, this year!—the schools had given up attempting to continue classes. Life had been reduced to simple survival. Scraping together enough food to eat one more meal. Enough clean water to drink, cook, and wash. Avoiding the bombs one more day and one more night.

We still had potatoes to eat, thanks to the winter supply in our basement bin. But there was little else left in the shops, even if we'd had money to buy it. Butcher shops, bakeries, grocers—all had empty shelves if indeed they were not already rubble. By Christmas, most shops had simply closed their doors.

In any case, there were few people left in the city. Since the first bombings, there'd been a mass exodus, anyone who could take shelter with family or friends in safer parts of Germany. This included Tante Klarla, whom we'd visited after the first bombing, and most of my other relatives. My grandparents moved just outside the city where they had a small shack on a garden plot. I am assuming Lisbeth and I stayed because we had no place to go, though I was never told why we couldn't join my grandparents or other relatives.

Tante Friedel and my cousin Ruth also remained in the apartment building where I'd taken shelter from the first bomb attack. If running into their basement had been my first turning point in life, our escape from death in the caves on Christmas night was what I would from that moment forward consider my second turning point. I did not yet know much about God. But I knew beyond a shadow of doubt that I had been miraculously spared. And if that was true, then Someone had spared me, and it had been for a reason. And that in turn meant that I, Eleanor, was not just some accidental configuration of DNA code, as our Nazi teachers taught, or an unwanted, castaway child, but a person whose life had value and a purpose.

Where did I get such thoughts as a frightened, lonely ten-year-old? Simple. Even though I did not yet know Him, the Lord God already had His hand on me and was speaking to my heart. I emphasize this because sometimes when we witness to others about our faith, we are distressed or disheartened if they don't immediately respond. But the truth is that unless God has already touched their hearts, the words we say will not make an impact. We can be a link in someone finding God. But we cannot force anyone to believe. Like a divine gardener preparing fertile soil, God was working in my heart so that it would be ready when the time came to plant the seeds of His Word.

Not that I ever spoke such thoughts aloud. I never pursued with Lisbeth her comment about God. As we climbed back up the cobble-stone street under a dawn sky hazy with smoke and dust that Christmas morning, we saw bomb damage everywhere. But when we reached our own apartment building, it was still standing.

Going inside, we had our normal holiday celebration as though we had not just narrowly escaped death. But the decorated tree, dollhouse, my doll with its new outfit, even the few holiday goodies Lisbeth had been able to scrounge up, brought me no joy. In fact, I don't remember ever again after that day playing with the dollhouse or any other toy. My childhood was over. My only thought was staying alive.

Shortly after the Christmas bombing, Lisbeth and I abandoned our apartment to move in with Tante Friedel and my cousin Ruth down in the city market district. Like Lisbeth's husband, my uncle Wilhelm had been killed in the fighting in Russia. With worsening odds of surviving the continued bombing, Lisbeth and Tante Friedel decided they might as well pool resources and live together—or die together!

Tante Friedel's apartment was similar to ours with just two rooms—a kitchen and a bedroom where two beds were set up. I shared one bed with Lisbeth, and Ruth shared another with her mother. As I've already described, the toilets were down in the courtyard. One bakery still remained nearby, and we would get up in the morning, go to the bakery for fresh rolls, which we would eat with coffee for our breakfast.

Then Lisbeth and Tante Friedel would leave for work at the bandage factory.

My own memories of this time are a jumble. But my cousin Ruth told me in later years that I was a very nervous, alert child, always standing at the window listening for bombs and sirens. I also started walking in my sleep, coming to my senses only when Lisbeth discovered my absence and would shake me awake. The apartment door was kept locked, or who knows what peril I might have walked into unknowing.

One morning, I woke up unusually early. The others were still sound asleep. Going to the window, I looked out. Everything appeared normal, but something in my heart, some strange feeling squeezing my stomach, told me, *You have to get out of here today!* As at the caves on Christmas night, I heard no audible words, but the sense of urgency was so strong that I rushed into the bedroom.

"Get up! Get up!" I cried out, shaking the others awake. "We have to leave town now! Quick! Quick! Get dressed!"

What I never really thought about at the time, but amazes me when I look back on that day, is that no one argued with me. They clambered out of bed and quickly got dressed. Lisbeth and Tante Friedel threw some supplies in shoulder bags. We all grabbed bottles filled with vinegar to carry with us. This might seem an odd thing to a twenty-first century reader. But at the time, German citizens were taught that sniffing vinegar would ward off the fumes of mustard gas or other chemical weapons. Of course, this turned out to be another Nazi lie, but carrying around vinegar bottles helped keep the population calm.

By this point, I was urging the others to hurry. "We have to go now! We can't wait any longer!"

It was just past dawn by the time we were outside and hurrying down the street that led out of town. The urgency in me had not eased, but was increasing. I kept telling the others to walk faster. Many years later, I asked my cousin why they all listened and obeyed me.

"There was something about you, Eleanor," she told me. "When you said something, it was like you were receiving it from somewhere else. We had no choice but to listen."

I know now it was God's voice warning me. But Lisbeth and Tante Friedel didn't believe in God or superstitions of any sort either. Perhaps it was as simple as Lisbeth remembering that I'd been right about the caves on Christmas. Either way, they obediently quickened their steps to keep up with me as I hastened my own pace. Once out of the city, the street turned into a country road lined with shady trees. I didn't let the others slow down. We walked for several hours. By noon, we'd reached a village with an inn. We were very thirsty as well as tired, so we approached the inn.

"We've walked here from the city," Lisbeth explained to the proprietor. "Would you be able to share some water with us?"

"Certainly. We have a well right over there." The proprietor pointed out a pump in the yard, then offered us some tin cups. "Here. Take these and help yourself."

We pumped water into the cups and drank. After the long walk, it was the most delicious water I could remember. Right near the pump was a lushly green wooded area filled with pine trees. We settled there to rest. The urgency that had kept me moving was gone, and I was content to sit there, sipping the cool, refreshing well water and breathing deeply of air that held no hint of smoke or burnt gunpowder, but only the tangy freshness of pine sap.

But just as we'd all begun to relax, we heard the drone of planes approaching overhead. I could hear the laboring of their engines, signifying a heavy load. Lisbeth jumped to her feet, urging us all to scramble deeper under the trees where we couldn't be seen from above. Scooting into the underbrush, we lay flat and still. It was too late to escape. We'd just have to hope they wouldn't waste bombs on such a small village.

Sure enough, the planes quickly receded into the distance. But more were following behind. As always, I occupied myself counting the winged shapes as they passed. Twenty. Fifty. Seventy. By the time I quit counting, at least a hundred planes had passed overhead. And all of them were heading in the direction from which we'd come!

"Eleanor, I've lost my watch!" Lisbeth whispered to me frantically over the noise of the aircraft. "I think I must have left it at the well when we were getting water. We have to get it back."

Where I was stretched out, my head was very close to my aunt's lap. The final wave of planes had swept overhead, the roar of their engines dwindling into the distance until I could hear a quiet tick-ticking. I whispered back to my aunt, "No, I can hear your watch ticking."

Lisbeth fumbled around until she found the watch tucked into a pocket. When she pulled it out, I could see that it was 12:30 p.m., only a half-hour since we'd reached the village. We finally got up and started back down the road toward Plauen. I've described before how Plauen sits in a natural basin surrounded by hills. So when we reached a ridge where the road led down out of the surrounding hills into the valley, we could see all of Plauen laid out in front of us. The city was in flames.

Mobs of people fleeing the city engulfed us as we continued down the road into the valley. Lisbeth and Tante Friedel engaged a number in conversation. They all told the same story. The entire center of the city was destroyed, the central market bombed completely flat. If we hadn't left the city that morning, we would have retreated to Tante Friedel's basement when the air raid started. Which meant we would all be dead, if her building had indeed been destroyed.

I saw Lisbeth and Tante Friedel exchange stunned glances. Then they both turned to stare at me. Neither said anything about my strange prescience that had saved all our lives. I didn't either. I just tucked away in my heart the assurance that once again Someone had intervened to spare my life and that of my family.

CHAPTER EIGHT

AFTERMATH

God is our refuge and strength, an ever-present help in trouble. Therefore we will not fear, though the earth give way and the mountains fall . . .

—Psalm 46:1-2a

T he sun was now setting. We didn't dare go into the city center, still billowing columns of smoke and fire. We prowled around the outskirts, searching for a safe place to shelter for the night. We finally found an empty building. The door stood open, and all the windows were blown out. Inside, there were some tables. I still remember the feel of crunched glass under my sleeve as I wiped off the tables, which became our bed for the night.

The next morning, we pressed on as far as we could into the city. As we'd been told, nothing in the city center had survived the bombing. We were left literally with the clothes on our back and the few odds and ends Lisbeth and Tante Friedel had packed for our trek. Tante Friedel and Ruth left Plauen immediately after. After Uncle Wilhelm died, Tante

Friedel had acquired a male friend who lived in a different town, and that was where they went.

Once again, Lisbeth and I had no place to go, so we stayed in the ruined city. We found temporary refuge with a relative of Tante Friedel, a widow with ten children, whose small apartment on the very edge of Plauen had survived the bombing. The area where she lived on the city outskirts was actually Plauen's garden sector. People living downtown would rent or buy a garden plot there, which they would visit all summer to grow vegetables for eating, canning, or selling in the market.

Like my two uncles, the widow's husband had died fighting in Russia. The apartment was even more cramped than Tante Friedel's had been. I shared a bed with seven other children, all of us sleeping sideways across the lumpy mattress. We were also further from the city center, which meant a longer trek to take shelter in the caves. Since the city's electrical grid had been destroyed, there were no longer air raid sirens to give warning of approaching bombers. Instead, we strained our ears constantly for the rumble of aircraft, upon which we would race for shelter.

With no electricity and the factories all destroyed, there were no longer any jobs for Lisbeth or anyone else. We now spent our days hovering near the caves, ready to duck inside. Many of the city's small remnant no longer bothered seeking shelter, feeling they were all going to be killed eventually, so why not get it over with. In contrast, I felt more confident with every passing month and close brush with death that I was destined to survive the war, so I no longer worried about it.

The last major bombing of Plauen took place on April 10th, 1945. The date is significant because my cousin Christa was born to my uncle Eric and his wife Elsa just one day earlier. My father's two brothers, Eric and Kurt, had moved to New Jersey at the same time as my father. Sometime after Hitler's rise to power, but before the outbreak of WWII in September, 1939, both brothers had moved back to Germany. Uncle Eric had either been wounded or had some other disability that kept him from fighting. He and Elsa already had six children, and Elsa was pregnant with another. Their neighborhood was quite distant from the city center and to this point had survived the bombings.

As with all my paternal relatives, I had never really known Onkel Eric's family, but in later years I was told the story of that night. Tante Elsa was delivered of a healthy, strong baby daughter on April 9th. The next day began the worst bombing attack Plauen had yet endured. Those outlying parts of the city still standing were almost completely flattened, including the neighborhood where Onkel Eric and Tante Elsa lived. Someone managed to get word to my paternal grandfather that his son had a new baby girl.

As soon as the bombing stopped, my grandfather and some other family members headed into Plauen to look for Eric and Elsa (that they never bothered looking for their other granddaughter, me, is something I've refused to let bother me). They found the four-story apartment where Eric and his family lived sliced in half as though by a knife instead of a bomb. Along with survivors of other families in the building, they began digging through the rubble. One by one, bodies were uncovered. Among them were Onkel Eric, Tante

Elsa, their six children, and even the midwife. But they found no sign of a newborn baby.

With all the chaos, you can imagine that just finding out who was dead and who still lived was a major difficulty for the citizens of Plauen. To facilitate communication, a large tree that had survived the destruction in downtown Plauen was designated the city post office. People would nail messages to the tree. Others would come to the tree, looking to see if missing family members had left a notice there. My grandfather left a note there, asking for any information on a newborn baby found in the general vicinity of Eric and Elsa's apartment.

A month later, a Red Cross nurse spotted the note and contacted my grandfather. "Hello, I have that baby you're asking about."

The nurse told how she'd been walking home through the debris after the bombing. She'd heard a baby crying, which seemed impossible since the entire neighborhood was in ruins. She started picking up boards and bricks, trying to trace where the sound was coming from. Finally, she looked up. Across the street from the rubble that had been my uncle's apartment building was a similar building that was badly damaged, but still standing. Thrusting out of the third floor were two wooden beams with enough linoleum floor still stretching between them to hold a baby carriage. The frantic cries of an infant were coming from the baby carriage, which was literally suspended over empty space.

The nurse ran back to the makeshift Red Cross office where she'd been working to get help. She then climbed up over the debris until she reached the third floor. There she dug a hole in the debris big enough to pull the carriage in from its precarious perch. Inside the carriage she found a newborn baby. No other survivors had been found, so no one knew whose family the baby belonged to. The nurse and her husband had never been able to have children, so she decided this baby was God's gift for them to raise. She took the baby home and had been caring for her ever since.

The nurse asked if she and her husband could formally adopt baby Christa. My grandparents agreed so long as they could be part of her life. Christa grew up, married, and had three children of her own. I was privileged to meet her decades later when I returned to Plauen. She and her husband Gottfried are devout Christians and very active in their church. Like my own near-brush with death, there is no rational explanation why Christa survived when no one else in that building did—except that God had a purpose for her life that was not yet complete. Such stories are always a reminder to me that to understand God's dealings in our lives we need to go beyond our intellect into something called faith!

I have my own vivid memory of that final, terrible air raid. It was early afternoon when the bombing started. Food had been growing more and more scarce, and Lisbeth and I were standing in a bread line, waiting patiently with a long line of other hungry residents for a small loaf to stave off our hunger through the night. Suddenly, fighter planes dove in low over the crowd, a rat-tat-tat of machine gun fire drowning out their engines as they fired into the bread line. People were falling everywhere, their clothing turning bright red from blood as bullets tore into their flesh.

Lisbeth grabbed my hand, and we sprinted for shelter. As we ran, I experienced the most beautiful vision. It couldn't have lasted for more than a few seconds, but it was so vivid that I never forgot the details. There was bright sunshine, a beautiful park, lots of trees, and benches. In the vision I was grown up, and sitting with me on one of the benches were people talking about God. Even as we ran from the planes and the bullets, something in that vision spoke to me and said, "You are going to survive this, you are going to grow up, and someday I'm going to take you to this place of peace and beauty where you will know me."

Fast forward fifty years. My husband had passed away, and more recently, my mother-in-law had passed away too. Before her death, my mother-in-law and I had made reservations to visit Boca Raton, FL, famous for its Bible conference center and retirement village known colloquially as Bibletown. I decided to go anyway in tribute to my mother-in-law. While there, I was invited to visit for myself the condo complexes available for sale. An open house party was scheduled for Saturday. I accepted the invitation, and that Saturday I drove into the complex.

As I got out of my vehicle, I couldn't figure out what was rousing a strange feeling in me. The area was beautiful with a green lawn dotted with palms and flowering trees. Walkways meandered through quiet duplexes with gorgeous wrought-iron balconies. Residents were sitting here and there on benches, chatting happily and enjoying the fresh air. I looked up at the sky, then swiveled slowly to take in the panorama of grass, palm trees, benches.

Suddenly it hit me like a ton of bricks. This was my vision! This beautiful, peaceful place filled with people who loved and worshipped God was the exact image I'd been given all those years ago when I was once again running for my life. I ended up purchasing a condo there, which became my winter home for many years. In time, I had the privilege of sharing in Bibletown's large auditorium the story of my youth and of the vision God had given me of this place.

But back to that horrible spring day in Plauen when I could only cling to my confidence that I'd been chosen for a purpose and would somehow survive yet another day while so many others around me were dying. By April, 1945, the remaining residents of Plauen were aware that Hitler was losing his war. But as the bombers pounded the last standing neighborhoods into the ground, we had no idea how close the end was.

As it was, when the bombers left, their engines singing their relief at a lightened load, they never again returned. Day after day, night after night, we braced ourselves for renewed attacks. Instead, each night was quiet, and I found myself sleeping as undisturbed as is possible in a bed with seven other children. April passed into May. Then on May 8th, 1945, excitement swept through Plauen. Those who still had access to radios shared the newscasts with those who didn't. Germany's mighty military machine, the Wehrmacht, had not proved invincible after all, but had just surrendered unconditionally to the Allied forces. Hitler had taken the coward's way out by committing suicide.

Depending on who was listening, reactions ranged from ecstatic relief to dark despair. Most people were just glad to know the bombings were over and normal life could now begin anew. By that point, 3.4 million tons of explosives had fallen on Germany. What I remember of that day is climbing a hill not far from the tiny apartment where we lived with Tante Friedel's widowed relative and her ten children. The hill is called the Ostvorstaadt and is a landmark in Plauen. Nearby was one of the only churches to survive the bombings. As the news spread through the city, the church's bells began to ring, signifying an end to war and return to peace.

Many other residents had climbed the hill as well. We all stood there, listening to the bells chiming out their glad tidings and looking out over the rubble of what had been a beautiful city, saddened at the destruction, but relieved to be standing there alive. There were so few people left in the city by then that as we stood there, it felt we were a single brotherhood. People were embracing each other, exclaiming, "We did it! We survived! Where did you used to live? Oh, yes, I see! And you?"

For a brief respite, we looked at each other, exhausted, hungry, uncertain of the future, but rejoicing that peace had at last arrived. Then someone spoke loudly enough to be heard above the bells. "Well, we survived this war. But I think there's going to be another war, and this one is going to be between Russia and America."

It was as though the balloon of our gladness had just been punctured, draining out all the joy. We all looked at each other, and I knew we were thinking the same thing. *We cannot survive another war! We cannot face another war!*

But we would. In fact, the next war was already upon us. Not a war of bombers and machine guns. This would be a war of starvation.

Chapter Nine

Famine

He who dwells in the secret place of the Most High shall abide under the shadow of the Almighty.

—Psalm 91:1

The Americans rolled into town on the heels of Germany's surrender. Locals called it an invasion. The Americans called it a liberation. It was perhaps a bit of both.

By this time, spring had arrived. But all the bombing and devastation of war had disrupted the normal cycle of crop planting and food distribution. Instead of becoming more plentiful as summer progressed, food became increasingly scarce. I don't remember a single meal during that time, just always being hungry.

Food was strictly rationed—a pound of potatoes per person each week, an eighth-pound of margarine. Now there was an advantage to living among the abandoned garden plots, as we could at least glean vegetables there to stave off starvation. But that was soon gone, and displaced residents were pouring back into the city, putting an even greater strain on remaining resources. There were no more bread lines, but the American occupying force organized soup and water trucks. We would stand in line for a single cup of soup and cup of clean drinking water each day.

The American occupation was now full-blown. They'd established an army base nearby, and their convoys of jeeps sped through the city, tossing gum and chocolate bars into the crowds, which were highly prized. Unfortunately, the occupation and lack of food created another economy— prostitution. Young girls sought out the American soldiers, trading their bodies for a pound of coffee, nylons, chocolate, and other such rations. These became a post-war currency that could be traded for virtually any other need. Signs posted all over the city warned of the dangers of syphilis.

Many pregnancies followed these liaisons as well. If this seems immoral, it should be remembered that Hitler had taught German youth that breeding healthy Aryan babies outside of wedlock was not a sin, but a civic duty. While some girls married their American lovers, most eventually found themselves abandoned as the soldiers returned to their own countries. Most difficult were babies born whose fathers were African-American soldiers, since a generation of Germans raised on the propaganda of racial purity were hardly accepting of mixed-black children.

I remember a soldier trying to coax me to join him in exchange for chocolate. Not yet eleven years old, I was too innocent to really understand what I was being asked, but God protected me from any sexual abuse. I was far more interested that these strange soldiers filling our streets were from America, where I knew I'd been born. Somehow I got it into my head that one of these soldiers might even be my father.

I remember one soldier whose teeth and smile I decided looked just like mine. Seeking out my aunt, I told her, "Lisbeth, I think I just met my father!"

She began laughing. "Oh, Eleanor!"

My feelings hurt, I decided I would just pretend I had a father. Meanwhile, the Americans obviously ate well. It seemed to me there should be some advantage to having been born an American. One day I was so hungry I had been picking leaves from trees to fill my empty stomach. I had my birth certificate, since my mother had left all such paperwork with Lisbeth and Walter when she abandoned me. Digging it out of my aunt's belongings, I walked down to the American base.

By this time it was mid-morning. Locating the kitchen area, I walked up to a soldier. I showed him my birth certificate and said, "America!" Then I pointed to my mouth and queried, "Eat?"

The soldier knew no more German than I knew English. But he pointed at his watch, then held up five fingers. He was smiling, so I assumed he meant that I should come back at 5 p.m., when supper was served. I came back, but that soldier was gone, and when I showed my birth certificate to a new soldier, he chased me away. I left reluctantly, but I stopped to dig through several garbage cans that were outside the mess hall. In one of them were the scrapings from the soldiers' supper—rice, chicken, and cream sauce. The garbage can was almost full. With both hands, I began shoveling the food into my mouth. It was the best meal I could remember eating in a long time.

If I'd pursued my claim as an American citizen, perhaps the next few years would have been different. But I couldn't have known that, and after that day, I never bothered taking my birth certificate to the base again. Rationing continued, and so did our hunger. One byproduct of malnutrition and diminished health care was that virtually everyone suffered from parasites. Goiters were visible everywhere too from a lack of iodine in our diet.

At least jobs were again available, mostly carrying away rubble and cleaning up the streets. It was predominantly Plauen's women who picked up shovels and restored the city to some semblance of order. This was because their husbands, fathers, brothers, and sons were mostly dead. In my extended family, all the men had died except my paternal grandfather, including my uncle Eric and his six children in the bombing.

In September, the schools reopened. By now, residents had moved back from all the places where they'd taken refuge. Stores were reopening. We discovered that our old apartment building, from which we'd moved to Aunt Friedel's home, was still standing, so we moved back in.

Somewhere during this time period, my birth mother made contact with us. We were still constantly hungry, so when I received a small package all the way from America containing individually wrapped butterscotch candies, I was thrilled. I was also shocked to discover that the package was from my mother. I'd known I was born in America, but had no idea I still had a mother there. Lisbeth never explained why my mother was in America while I was in Germany. Over the next months, we received several more packages from my mother. One even had a birthday card addressed to me. On the cover was a well-fed, smiling American little girl in a pretty dress.

If it wasn't for such packages, many people might not have survived the following winter. I remember one family that had many relatives in America. They would receive packages almost every week. Emphasis was on high-calorie staples like chocolate, powdered milk, and Crisco. One day the family received a large package. They recognized all the contents except one small package with no label, but that appeared to contain some kind of dark dust.

"It must be something to eat, since they know how hungry we are," the mother finally announced. "Maybe it is ground-up nuts for protein. We'll make it into soup."

Taking a big pot, she grated rotting potatoes into it along with a few other ingredients and the package. The result was a reasonably tasty and filling supper for all, though it had a certain gritty aftertaste. Two weeks later, the family received a letter referencing the package.

"Everything is to eat, except for one package," the letter said. "Those are Grandmother's ashes. Please bury them in the cemetery next to Grandfather."

Which goes to show that when you're hungry enough, you'll eat anything! But if we thought starvation was the worst we now had to fear, we were about to learn otherwise. The American occupying force stayed in Plauen for just a few months. We would soon have given anything to have them back. I knew nothing then of what was happening in high places, but I would eventually learn how American president Harry Truman, British prime minister Winston Churchill, and Russian dictator Joseph Stalin sat down together to divide Germany into occupation zones.

The Americans staked out southern Germany, while the British took the northwest, which most closely approached their own borders. The French had done little to help win the war, but were eventually granted a small slice of territory as well. Meanwhile, the Russians ended up with northeastern Germany bordering Poland and northern Czechoslovakia, as well as access to the Baltic Sea. This included Plauen, which as I've mentioned is quite close to the border of Czechoslovakia. The division left Germany's capital, Berlin, deep into the Russian zone. But it too was divided into four sectors, one for each occupying force.

These divisions were intended to be temporary, but anyone who has studied history knows what happened next. Russia seized control of their zone, dividing Germany for the next four decades into two countries. The Berlin Airlift under American president Truman prevented the Russians from seizing the entire capital. But Berlin too would remain divided by its infamous wall until 1989, when German citizens responded to American president Ronald Reagan's unforgettable challenge to then-Russian leader Mikhail Gorbachev, "Mr. Gorbachev, tear down this wall!"

We, of course, had no idea at the time what was happening, only that in a single day, the Americans exited south out of Plauen while Russian troops poured in across the Czechoslovakian border. The Americans didn't go far. Plauen was only thirty kilometers from the Americans' new Air Force base in Hof, which in turn was less than five kilometers from the border between the American and Russian occupation zones. But to us, the American forces might as well have retreated back across the ocean. For just a few short months, Plauen had actually known freedom with no dictator ruling our lives. Now we were once again under a totalitarian regime—only now it was Stalin instead of Hitler.

When school started up again, we no longer had to learn Nazi propaganda. But now we had to study Russian language, history, and culture. Instead of a Nazi party member, now a Russian soldier sat in every classroom to ensure teachers were complying with the new regulations.

We were also now taught the truth of what Hitler and his Nazis had really done. We were shocked to learn about concentration camps. Under the Russians, we heard as little about the Jews as before. But we learned in detail about horrific Nazi atrocities such as tossing babies in the air to use as target practice, kicking pregnant women in the stomach, performing experimental surgery on prisoners without anesthesia. And, of course, the horrors of the gas chambers and other massacres. It became clear that these lessons were not designed for educational purposes, but to inflict punishment on German children for Hitler's assault on Russia.

Russian soldiers could also seize any property they wanted. Since so many German men were dead, a Russian soldier would simply move into a house and force the woman living there to serve as housekeeper and often bed partner as well. As under the American occupation, there were women who survived by catering to the soldiers. One woman in our apartment building simply switched from entertaining American officers to Russian, who paid her now in vodka and canned herring instead of coffee and nylons. We would see the soldiers coming and going with some envy as she never shared her largess with any of us.

Lisbeth and I sought food anywhere we could. Survival now was no longer about avoiding the bombs, but finding enough calories to fuel our bodies one more day. We had the contents of packages my mother had sent from America, so sometimes we would take the train into a farming region, where we would walk from farmhouse to farmhouse, asking if we could trade something from America for food. Lisbeth and I would set out in opposite directions with our scant inventory, then meet up at the end of the day to pool our earnings.

It was during these trips that I remember beginning to talk to my invisible Friend again, whom I now knew was the God who'd created this whole big world. I can remember saying, "God, we need to talk. You got me through the bombs. I haven't been abused by any soldier. But now I am very hungry, and I need your help. You have kept me alive to this point, and now you need to keep me alive with some food. When I get up to that house and knock on the door, please make them like me and give me a slice of bread. You can do that because you are very smart."

When I knocked on the door, a woman opened it. I showed her a scarf my mother had sent. "See, it has the Statue of Liberty on it from America. Would you like to trade it for some food?"

The woman took the scarf and exclaimed over how pretty it was. She also picked out a ball-point pen and some other items, then gave me a full loaf of bread, some baloney, and a small sack of grain. As I left, I raised my thoughts to my invisible Friend again. "Okay, God, you really did take care of me."

When I joined Lisbeth, I found out that she'd collected a portion of wheat grain and some other food stuffs. We would put the grain through our coffee grinder, for which we had no coffee, and make it into soup. The worst part was the train ride home because the Russian soldiers knew what we were doing, and they would always demand part of the food stuffs we'd garnered. Lisbeth taught me to hide what we'd glean under our clothing, but we still had to come up with something to pacify their demands.

Things did get better. Packages from my mother containing Crisco, salt, and other high-calorie items occasionally got through. We would go out into the fields around Plauen after harvest and glean any remaining grain or vegetables just like Ruth the Moabite in the Old Testament. My aunt Lisbeth was a wonder at stretching food. She made ersatz coffee out of chicory. A single potato grated with salt, pepper, and an egg made a delicious supper. Grain winnowed in a pillow case and ground up in the coffee grinder needed only water, salt, and a dab of Crisco to make an unleavened bread. That might not sound like much of a meal, but it filled our stomachs, and perhaps surprisingly, I was never sick.

But though my aunt took care of me physically, we still had no close mother-daughter relationship. There were no hugs or kisses nor praise for anything I did. We were just two people sharing a living space and working together to survive. I found myself turning more and more to my invisible Friend. When I retreated into my mind to talk to this Presence, it felt as though I was escaping within myself to a place very different from my war-devastated surroundings where I was protected and loved. Years later when I began reading the Bible, I came across a psalm that expressed what I felt when I stepped into that inner hidden space:

> He who dwells in the secret place of the Most High shall abide under the shadow of the Almighty. I will say of the Lord, "**He is** my refuge and my fortress; my God, in Him I will trust
>
> —Psalm 91:1-2

I knew nothing then about religion. I'd never attended a church. But like King David when he wrote this psalm, somehow I knew that somewhere out there was a sanctuary where the Creator of this universe dwelt, and if I could just retreat to that secret place, I would find there refuge, protection, and even love, no matter my chaotic outward circumstances.

Chapter Ten

A Dark Dungeon

I have loved you with an everlasting love

—Jeremiah 31:3

Even as Plauen was becoming functional again under the Russians, another change brought fresh upheaval into my fragile subsistence. Lisbeth had returned to work at the factory, which now produced towels, linens, and other household products instead of bandages for troops. She also acquired a male friend, who like Lisbeth had lost his spouse during the war.

Her male friend usually visited our apartment on weekends, so I think he must have lived and worked in another city. He always brought food, for which I was thankful. They would kiss and cuddle while Lizbeth cooked him a nice supper. Then she would send me into the bedroom and lock the door. We had no electricity, so I was left in absolute darkness.

Out in the kitchen, Lisbeth would tune the radio to Johann Strauss waltzes or other dance music. I could hear them laughing, talking, kissing, dancing. Then there would be other sounds. They would spend the night on the sofa. When her friend left in the morning, Lisbeth would unlock the door and let me out.

I cannot describe just how frightened, abandoned, and alone I felt every time I heard that key turn in the lock. I would crawl into the bed and curl up in a fetal position, pulling the covers over my head to drown out the noises that came through the wall. It was also very cold, since the only heat in the apartment came from the iron stove in the kitchen. Lying there in the smothering dark, a prisoner behind a locked door, felt even worse to me than running from the bombs. I had not heard Lisbeth laugh or sound so carefree since Uncle Walter went away to war. That she would kiss and hug this stranger, yet never lavished any affection on me, hurt me deeply.

It was at this point that I came to the realization I was truly alone in this world. By now I knew that I had a mother and father in America who didn't want me. Now the woman who'd been the only mother I knew didn't seem to care about me at all. So I came to the conclusion that I must be a very bad, worthless girl, since no one wanted me. My pain was mixed in with fear. What if Lisbeth abandoned me as my parents had? What would become of me?

My only escape was to retreat once again to that secret place in my mind. My parents had not loved me. Lisbeth didn't love me anymore, if she ever had. But I clung to the assurance that this invisible Presence did care about me. If not, why had my life been spared? Lying there in the dark, I would visualize myself in that beautiful, secret place and speak to my invisible Friend.

I can't see you or touch you, so I have to make believe you exist, I thought into the darkness. *But I know you are real, and you are the only one who cares for me and loves me.*

This went on weekend after weekend. Then Lisbeth told me to pack my bag because I was going to be sent away for two weeks. I wasn't the only child going. It was part of some program set up to send undernourished city children who'd survived the bombings to the countryside, where they would spend two weeks with an assigned farm family and be fattened up with nourishing food and milk.

Lisbeth packed my bag and took me to the train. Quite a number of other children had also gathered for the trip. Only when it was time to board did I learn that she wasn't coming with me. She told me my foster family would pick me up at the other end and put me back on the train in two weeks to come home. Then she turned and left without so much as a goodbye. I had never in my memory been apart from Lisbeth for even a single night, and I was petrified as the train pulled away from the station.

When we arrived, I followed the other children, clutching my bag tight. A crowd of foster parents was waiting to pick up the children. I watched as, one by one, the name of a child was announced. A couple would approach, pick up the child's suitcase, and carry them off with hugs and smiles. But no one said my name. At last, the final child had been called, and I was left alone on the train station. Finally, a man walked up to me.

"Are you waiting for your family to pick you up?" he asked. I nodded a mute yes. He went on, "Well, don't be surprised if they are late. The family assigned to you didn't want to be part of this program, so who knows if and when they might come."

What was I supposed to say to that? I sat on the platform for what seemed hours, and still no one came. As had become my habit, I retreated inside myself and began praying. *God, it's okay if these people don't want me because you want me. You didn't let me die in war. You are my friend. My best friend. So it's okay, even if they don't come and I stay here all night.*

Already, I was feeling better. I took a deep breath and settled myself into my seat. But just as I did so, the family assigned to me showed up. There was an older man and a younger man with his wife and baby. As I'd been warned, they were not friendly and didn't look happy to see me. But the younger man picked up my suitcase, and I followed them to their house.

The only good part about the visit was the food, of which there was plenty as promised. Otherwise, they ignored me. I was assigned to watch the baby, so I spent all day wheeling the baby carriage between the house and barn or sitting in the garden, listening to cows moo and watching the chickens running around. At night, I retreated to the narrow cot I'd been assigned in the attic, which was a hot, tiny space under a steeply slanted roof. I was deeply unhappy. I'd never been away from Lisbeth so long, much less with strangers.

Four days into my assigned week, I was out in the garden with the baby carriage when someone called, "Eleanor, is that you?"

A woman had approached the front gate. I was stunned to recognize her as my friend Maria's mother. I hadn't seen her or Maria since the bombing raids had shut our school down. I hurried over to the gate, but I couldn't get it open. Maria's mother smiled at me and asked kindly, "How are you doing, Eleanor?"

I burst into tears. Between my sobs, I told her how unhappy I was. I couldn't understand how she'd found me. She told me that Maria was in the same program and had been assigned to a nearby farm. She'd come up to visit her daughter. This made me cry even harder, since I hadn't realized that family members could visit if they wanted.

Maria's mother finally left to see her daughter. But a few days later, she returned to visit Maria again. She stopped by to see me, and I must have still been very distraught because she told me, "Why don't you come home with me? I'll take you to your aunt."

The family made no objection to my leaving early, so I gathered my things and went with Maria's mother. When she dropped me off at our apartment, I could see that Lisbeth's male friend had clearly been staying there while I was gone. I thought my aunt would be happy to see me. Instead she was furious.

"What is the matter with you?" she yelled at me. "Are you so weak you couldn't stick it out a few more days? Why can't you be strong?"

I didn't answer, knowing that she'd be angry, no matter what I said. She didn't ask me ever what had happened there or why I'd come home. I had missed her terribly, but she, who had cared for me and never been apart from me since I was two years old, showed no pleasure at having me home, only annoyance that I'd interrupted her time alone with her male friend. I felt even more unwelcome and unloved. Once again, I found myself locked in at night.

Some years ago, after the fall of the Soviet Union and reunification of Germany made travel to eastern Germany possible again, I was privileged to return to Plauen, where I visited fifty or more of my relatives who still live there. Among them was my cousin Ruth, Tante Friedel's daughter, who was two years younger than me. She invited me to stay in her apartment, insisting that I as her guest take her bedroom while she slept on the couch.

As I lay there in the darkness, the oddest feeling came over me. Suddenly, I realized that this bedroom, in fact, the entire apartment, was an exact replica of the one where Lisbeth and I had lived. The door between me and the kitchen where my cousin slept was identical to the one my aunt had locked to keep me from interrupting her activities with her male friend.

I began praying as the darkness pressed in, causing a familiar feeling of loneliness and abandonment to sweep over me. I reminded myself that I hadn't been truly alone in that darkness because God was with me, protecting me. It was in that moment, like a flash of lightning illuminating my soul, that I realized I had it all wrong. That turned key in the lock was not to keep me a prisoner, but to protect me. I was not locked in. Rather, all that was happening in that other room was locked out. God had provided me a sanctuary, protecting me by that locked door.

And maybe that had been Lisbeth's intention in making sure I was locked away from any contact with her male visitors, this one and others that followed. I came to understand in later years, as I didn't then, that Lisbeth's laughter and flirting might have been more about providing for the two of us and staving off starvation than any genuine carefreeness. Maybe in her own way she really did care about me, even if she did not feel the emotional bond of a mother, and locking me behind that door was the best way she could show it.

As the realization swept over me, I jumped out of Ruth's bed, rushed over, and kissed the door, giving thanks to God. I, who'd felt myself such an unloved child, suddenly felt so loved. A Bible verse that had become one of my favorite scriptures came to my mind as I slipped back into bed:

> The Lord appeared to us in the past saying: "I have loved you with an everlasting love; I have drawn you with unfailing kindness."
>
> —Jeremiah 31:3

Yes, God's unfailing kindness and everlasting love had been there in my past, even when I didn't recognize it, and His love will remain with me forever.

CHAPTER ELEVEN

TYRANNY RETURNS

He [Jehovah] will command his angels concerning you to guard you in all your ways.

—Psalm 91:11

I'd turned eleven years old shortly after the Russians took control of Plauen and the rest of eastern Germany. By this age, I was an odd mixture of world-weary and naïve. I'd witnessed more ugliness in my short life than most readers today could imagine. I was not unaware of what went on between Lisbeth and her male friend on the opposite side of that locked bedroom door. Nor was I unaware of why certain young German women in our apartment building or walking the streets with their soldier boyfriends looked so much better fed than the rest of us.

And yet Lisbeth had done better in shielding me than I'd perhaps thought because I was also quite naïve about such "adult" activities. One of my regular duties at this time was to get up in the middle of the night with my aunt. Pulling a small wagon with wheels or a sled during winter, we would sneak out of town to the surrounding forests. There we cut up branches and small trees for firewood, tying it onto the sled or wagon to drag home.

I didn't really understand why we did this at night, but I know now that gathering firewood from public forests was against the law. That firewood was our only source for heat as well as cooking, so we paid no attention to regulations laid down by officials who lived warm, well-fed lives. Another of my chores was to get up early each morning, chop the wood into smaller pieces, then build a fire in our three-tiered iron stove, using newspaper for kindling. In winter, my breath made a white fog as I struggled to light the fire, and the kitchen window would be so completely frosted over, you couldn't see outside.

Of course, all our neighbors were doing the same. One day, a man from one of the other apartments approached me, saying, "Eleanor, you are such a hardworking little girl. Why don't you go with me up into the woods after school today? We can gather kindling, enough for your apartment and mine, maybe even for the whole building. We can pile the extra here in the entry so everyone can help themselves. Would you like to help me do that?"

"Sure, that would be nice!" I responded. The man seemed kindly, one of the few who'd ever taken an interest in me. My thought was that he knew I didn't have a father of my own, so he wanted to be nice to me. And gathering firewood by daylight would certainly be easier than our midnight treks.

Lisbeth was still at work when I arrived home from school. The man was waiting for me, so I walked with him up the hillside into the woods. I immediately saw downed branches and sapling pines that were perfect for firewood, so I was surprised when he didn't stop. He kept walking further and further into the woods. I didn't want to cause trouble, so I followed at his heels without voicing my confusion.

We eventually reached a small clearing. I'd seen others in the woods gathering firewood, but here there was no one in sight. The man suddenly put his arms around me and started kissing me. Again, I was so naïve I didn't understand what was happening. I remember thinking this must be how a daddy shows his little girl that he likes her. This man clearly wanted to be a surrogate father to a little girl who had none of her own.

The man then told me to lie down on the grass, so we could take a little rest after our long walk before starting work. It was when he started touching me in areas I'd never been touched that I began to feel uncomfortable. But I still didn't want to offend this fatherly man who'd been so kind to me. Unbuttoned his trousers, he began stretching himself across my prone frame. He was heavy, his breath unpleasant, making me even more uncomfortable.

Just at that moment, a babble of laughter and talking broke the solitude of the clearing. It sounded like a group of people climbing the hillside for an outing or picnic. The man immediately scrambled to his feet. Buttoned his trousers, he hastily began picking up branches and scraps of other wood. I calmly got to my feet, straightened my clothing, and went to work as well. He made no effort to touch me again, and I returned home happy to have a nice supply of firewood.

The man didn't invite me to go wood-cutting again, and shortly after that incident, Lisbeth and I moved from Plauen. It was years later before it dawned on me what he'd been about to do. God had not just saved me from bombs and starvation, but from sexual abuse. I am reminded of another portion of Psalm 91, one of my favorite Scripture passages.

> If you say, "The Lord is my refuge," and you make the Most High your dwelling, no harm will overtake you, no disaster will come near your tent. For he will command his angels concerning you to guard you in all your ways.

> —Psalm 91:9-11

Certainly, there were angels watching over me that day to protect me from that man's ill intent. By this time, I'd also met another person who became a refuge during our remaining time in Plauen. I was now in the fifth grade. My teacher, Frau Benner, was a widow with one daughter, then eight years old. She took a liking to me and would invite me to her apartment at least once a month for tea.

Perhaps she too was aware that I had no mother of my own or felt that I was a little neglected. I don't know, but I was grateful for her attention. A highly educated, intelligent woman, she was always well-dressed with very elegant manners. We would sit in her living-room on opposite sides of a small table where she'd set out the tea paraphernalia and discuss a wide range of topics. Her daughter was also nice, though too young to become my close friend.

Frau Benner quickly became my model. She was so warm and loving to me. She would hug me as my aunt never did. As with my friend Marie, I felt immediately at home in the tasteful, quiet order of her apartment and its scholarly environment. She was not religious, as far as I know, and never spoke of God. But she did encourage me to pursue learning, excellence, and beauty in life. Her home became another crack of light into my dungeon of darkness and abandonment, showing me that I could aspire to a better life than the one I was living with Lisbeth, who now seemed always angry with me and interested only in her boyfriends.

By this time Lisbeth had broken up with her original male friend. Or perhaps he had simply moved to another city. A series of men moved in and out of our lives before she found another more permanent friend. One of the few activities Lisbeth and I still did together was gleaning in the fields. Rising very early, we would walk into the countryside where there were fields of potatoes, barley, wheat, and corn.

Since food remained scarce and rationed, policemen were stationed to guard the harvest. One policeman in particular was assigned to fields where Lisbeth and I gleaned. Lisbeth would flirt with the policeman, whose name was Hans Leksa. Then he'd ignore us as we headed into the field, using the large aprons we wore as basins to hold whatever foods we could scrounge up that the harvesters had missed.

Then one day, Hans came to our apartment, bearing gifts of food. A short time later, Hans and Lisbeth were married. Around the same time, Hans was reassigned to a new duty posting in a town called Bad Elster thirty kilometers south of Plauen. Now that Lisbeth had married Hans, this meant we had to relocate as well. I was devastated to leave Plauen. In tears, I made the rounds, saying goodbye to Maria and other school friends. The hardest goodbye was Frau Benner. She assured me that I could come back and visit any time I returned to Plauen. But that did not console me.

Bad Elster turned out to be a small, picturesque spa town of about three thousand in population nestled among heavily wooded hills on the border between Bavaria and Czechoslovakia. The reason for its serene beauty was because the Allies had chosen it as an invasion point into Germany, so it had been spared the bombings that destroyed Plauen and other cities. Hans Leksa had an almost-grown daughter named Ruth, perhaps 17-18 years old, who moved with us. When the four of us arrived in Bad Elster, we discovered that our new home was actually a border station called Barenlow where the road from Bad Elster crossed into Czechoslovakia. A dilapidated two-story building had been divided into apartments for border police and their families. Ours was on the second floor, and from its window, I could see a barricade across the road. On the other side was Czechoslovakia.

I came to know every inch of the road into Bad Elster once school started. It was about an hour's walk into the town center. Some of the other border police were also married, but the other children in our building were all babies, so I walked to and from school alone. I left each morning at 7 a.m. Classes ran from 8 a.m. to noon, then from 3-6 p.m. So I would walk an hour home for lunch, eat, then walk back in time for afternoon classes, returning home again at 6 p.m.

This added up to four hours each day, which was quite tiring for an eleven-year-old. Especially since there was still not enough food to fuel all that exercise. I'm not sure why it occurred to no one, including me, to let me take a lunch pail so I could rest in town during the afternoon break. But that was just the way things were.

Still, there were advantages to my new circumstances. The woods between our home and Bad Elster were thick, tall, and majestically beautiful. Soaring pines gave off oxygen so rich and clean it was intoxicating. Blueberry bushes grew thick, and when they were ripe, I would stop to stuff my face, the sweet, purplish globules exploding deliciously in my mouth. Bird songs, squirrels scampering up tree trunks, and the occasional glimpse of other animals added to my delight. The woods in winter were just as beautiful with drifts of sparkling-white snow and lacy frost patterns transforming the underbrush to a fairy wonderland.

Even my solitude became something I cherished. It was so peaceful walking alone through such a beautiful example of God's creation. I knew such splendid grandeur could not be here by random accident, as the Nazis and Russians both taught. Someone had created this paradise. With so much time alone to think, I found myself pondering deep thoughts about life and how I had come to be and what was the purpose of this world and my life.

That led me to direct my thoughts again to the invisible Presence I'd come to count as my only true friend. It was an easy leap to conclude that the invisible Presence who had kept me from death during the war was also the One smart and powerful enough to create this beautiful world I was seeing all around me. In Romans 1:20, the apostle Paul reminds us that:

> Since the creation of the world God's invisible qualities—his eternal power and divine nature— have been clearly seen, being understood from what has been made, so that people are without excuse.

Hundreds of years earlier, King David expressed the same truth in one of his psalms:

> The heavens declare the glory of God; the skies proclaim the work of his hands. Day after day they pour forth speech; night after night they reveal knowledge. They have no speech, they use no words; no sound is heard from them. Yet their voice goes out into all the earth, their words to the ends of the world.
>
> —Psalm 19:1-4

I might not have known yet who God was or even what He was. But in the quiet, beautiful creation through which I walked each day, I saw clearly the work of a Creator. And through that work, I was coming to understand something of the nature of God. A Person who could create all I saw must possess great power. He must also be very beautiful for the world He'd created to be so beautiful. And to pour out such varied bounty of color, scents, tastes, the music of birdsong and brook, on small, undeserving human beings like myself surely demonstrated nothing short of immeasurable love.

I in turn felt my child's heart swell with love and gratitude towards my smart, loving, invisible Friend as I drank in the magnificent splendor of each passing season. I know now that God was drawing me to Himself, not just through the beauty of Nature, but through the rejection, loneliness, and hardship that filled my days.

So, let's talk about Loneliness for a minute, my friend...

If you are in the Dungeon of Loneliness right now and are gripping the bars in desperation to get out, STOP. Embrace your loneliness, and you will find that it is a spiritual tool in the hand of God to pull you gently into His Presence in intimacy. It can be beautiful. By the way, we were created for this purpose.

Whether you are married or single, alone or in a crowd, loneliness can strike without warning. When that happens, remember it is a nudge from God to make you focus on Him, your Creator. One of the psalms explains this so well...

> He that dwells in the secret place of he most High,
>
> shall abide under the shadow of the Almighty.
>
> —Psalm 91:1

So Loneliness is a spiritual gift from your Creator to force you into going outside of yourself into Him, Who is the Source of all we need. Loneliness is not a lack of people in our lives. It is a feeling of being disconnected not only from the world and reality, but also from ourselves. In Genesis chapter 3, Adam and Eve experienced this. After they disobeyed God's command, they instantly became separated from Him in fellowship and so covered themselves. This is called Religion. God is not religious. He is the great Lover of all of us. It says in Hebrews:

> I will never leave you nor forsake you.
>
> —Hebrews 13:5

What a satisfying and fulfilling relationship this can be when we listen to the pain of our loneliness. I have experienced this all my life.

So folks...there is a difference between loneliness and solitude. Loneliness is something we run from, but solitude is something we seek for refreshment when we are hurting.

Chapter Twelve

Father to the Fatherless

His faithfulness will be your shield and rampart.
You will not fear the terror of night . .

—Psalm 91:4b-5a

My passage alone through the woods was not always so peaceful. Once winter set in, nightfall came long before I started home from school in the evenings. There were no street lights, and only a rare vehicle or bike ever passed, so the darkness was absolute, and only the feel under my shoes of the road's well-worn ruts kept me from getting lost.

To make things more frightening, I didn't always have the road to myself. This was a main route for people attempting to escape East Germany into Czechoslovakia, which at that time was still a strong democracy closely allied with Western Europe and the United States. This would end with the communist coup that took control in February, 1948, bringing Czechoslovakia under Soviet control for the next four decades. But at this point, Germans wanting to escape to the west often did so by crossing into Czechoslovakia. So

Russian troops patrolled border territories, including the road I walked to school.

One evening as I was walking home, there was still enough light for me to see a Russian soldier jump out a ditch ahead of me, cradling a machine gun. I was terrified, since the Russians shot or arrested anyone they suspected might be trying to escape. But I also knew there was no hope of escaping if I tried to run away. Desperation helped me formulate a quick plan. Banishing my fear from my face, I pasted in its place a big smile as I tried to walk naturally towards the soldier.

"*Zdrastvooyte!*" I greeted him in my best Russian. "I'm so glad to meet you."

As the soldier stared down at me, I pointed down the road, doing my best to prattle like a harmless, little girl. "I live down the road in that big house by the border crossing. I'm learning Russian in school. I come through here four times a day. Maybe I could practice my Russian with you. By the way, how is my Russian. Am I pronouncing it correctly?"

I don't know what the Russian soldier was thinking. He looked down at me as if to say, "You are one gutsy, little girl." Then he gave me a smile, lowered his gun, and let me pass. I never saw that particular soldier again, but I occasionally ran into other patrols. I would always put on a smile, greet them in Russian, and hope they could not read my mind to see how afraid I was.

I lived for two years there with Lisbeth, her husband Hans, and his daughter Ruth. I admired my new stepsister. Both she and my stepfather were far better educated than Lisbeth. They both liked to read books and the newspaper. Ruth shared books with me, taught me to do manicures, gave me tips on hygiene and grooming, and encouraged me to study hard.

"If you want to grow up to be a smart, successful woman," she told me, "you need to be educated. You need to love school."

Unfortunately, Lisbeth hated her stepdaughter passionately, and her marriage with Hans had become very tense. Part of this was because Ruth did none of the cooking, cleaning, or other household work, treating Lisbeth as though she were a servant there to wait on her. Ruth also brought home boyfriends, whom she would take to sleep in her bedroom, staying in there for days on end. They would wait until Lisbeth had gone shopping before sneaking out to raid the kitchen.

Lisbeth was always acutely aware that she didn't have the education or interest in books of her new husband's family. Her way to compete was by maintaining a spotless home. When Hans came home from his patrol shift, she would quickly hand me a broom or washrag and tell me to look busy, as though the sight of us always cleaning would impress him. Of course, it didn't, and Hans always took the side of his daughter in any disputes between them. Finally, the tension grew so strong that Ruth moved out, going off with one of her boyfriends.

By this time, I was enjoying a new adventure. Food remained scarce, especially with four of us in the household. One day Hans approached me. "Eleanor, if I help you cross over into Czechoslovakia, you can get enough food for all of us."

Hans explained his proposition. The border with Czechoslovakia was strictly patrolled. Anyone discovered crossing over was in danger of being shot. But a large German population lived in Czechoslovakia, three million in total, including the area across the border from Bad Elster. This had actually been Hitler's justification for invading Czechoslovakia, since Germany had considered the region part of its own territory until it was ceded in part to Czechoslovakia and the rest to Poland at the end of WW1.

Hans had acquaintances on the other side of the border who were as eager for such delicacies as vodka, smoked herring, and other Russian goods as Germans were for food products. Since he was a border policeman, it was simple enough to make contact at the barricade. But passing sizeable packages openly was out of the question. And an adult caught carrying a pack over the border would be arrested immediately. But no one would pay attention to a young girl out wandering the fields at night.

What Hans had in mind was for me to accompany him when he was on the night shift at the barricade, a period when there would be few other guards on duty. His responsibility was to patrol on foot along the border, which was just a stretch of woods with no fence except where the barricade went across the road. Once all was quiet and the night well advanced, I would slip past him across the border, carrying a backpack, and make my way to the farm where his contacts lived. I would spend the day there, then slip back again the next night, my backpack now filled with its return load.

I agreed unhesitatingly, flattered to be asked to help my family in such an important way. I felt no fear, perhaps because I had no concept of how dangerous it really was. I set out with my stepfather. At 2 a.m., he sent me across the border. I couldn't carry a flashlight for fear of Russian patrols. But Hans had pointed out to me a distant light that was my destination, and there was enough moonlight for me to pick my way through the fields. I hurried as fast as I could, slowing only when I was completely out of breath. I felt so grown-up, strong, and brave to be chosen for such a vital mission.

Just look at me! I told myself with pride. *I'll bet no one else in my school is doing this!*

Even with the distant light to focus on, finding my footing in the dark was not easy, and for a moment, I allowed the black, cold night to overwhelm me. But I quickly straightened up and made a deliberate choice to retreat to that secret place in my mind. I spoke to my invisible Friend as I continued forward.

You kept heavy bombs from falling on me. Saving my life was nothing to you because you are so smart and strong. If you could protect me from the bombs, you can get me safely across this border to get food for my family.

The reminder restored my courage. I continued toward the twinkle of light and found the house exactly as Hans had described. A family member who lived there was awake, waiting for me. I delivered my backpack, and he led me to a hay loft in the barn, where I went to sleep. Only later did I realize I'd been put in the barn so that if the Russians came searching, they could deny all knowledge of me.

The next day, I was fed as I hadn't been fed in months, including an entire egg for myself. In Germany, eggs were so rationed that I was fortunate to have one egg a year. The following night, the family loaded up my backpack with loaves of bread, wheat, grain, sardines, cheese, and salami. Hurrying back, I safely delivered my load to my stepfather.

My career as a border smuggler went on for quite some time. I became good friends with the German couple on the Czechoslovakian side. I also felt a new bond with my stepfather. I was still the little girl desperately seeking for someone to love me, and I was so happy that I'd managed to please him.

It was only when I became an adult, many years after I'd last seen Hans, that I realized how truly selfish his actions had been. He could have made the same trek as I did. Or if a girl would raise less suspicion, he could have sent his daughter Ruth exactly as he sent me. But he had no intention of risking his own life or his daughter's. So instead he sent a twelve-year-old girl. Far from choosing me because he cared about me or was proud of me, it was just the opposite. If I was shot or arrested, it would be no real loss to him.

Meanwhile, I was still spending four hours a day walking to and from school. That included Saturday, which was just a half-day of school. Visible from my school was a landmark that remains one of Bad Elster's best-known tourist attractions, *St. Trinitatis Kirche*, or the Lutheran Church of the Holy Trinity. German theologian Martin Luther had set in motion the Protestant Reformation on October 31, 1517, when he nailed to the door of the Wittenberg Castle church his 95 Theses, a list of questions and concerns related to corruption in the Catholic church, including the selling of indulgences purported to grant forgiveness of sin.

The Reformation reached Bad Elster in 1540, six years before Luther's death, with the installing of its first

Protestant pastor. In 1892, the original church was rebuilt as an imposing Gothic cathedral with tall bell-tower, vaulted cupola over the altar, and exquisite stained-glass windows. The doors of *St. Trinitatis* were kept unlocked during the day, and I often saw people going in and out. But I had not set foot in a church since my four-year-old debut as a flower girl.

One day instead of heading straight home after school, I walked over to the church. While I had no theological education, I somehow equated my invisible Presence with God because after we survived the first cave bombing my aunt said God didn't want us to die. I remember well my internal conversation as I walked up the steps and opened the heavy, carved-wood double doors. *God, I know you live in this big house called a church. Now I'm coming to visit you, and I'm going to make believe you are my vater (daddy). Is that okay? I don't have one, you know!*

Slipping quietly through the doors, I marveled at the vaulted ceiling far above me. The interior was dim, but multi-colored shafts of light filtering through stained-glass windows offered enough illumination to make out the length and breadth of the sanctuary. An aisle ran between two rows of polished wooden pews. Far above my head along three sides of the sanctuary ran an ornate balcony, also carved from a dark-hued stained wood.

At the front, I could see a flat, marble rectangle and another round marble receptacle. I would eventually learn that these were the altar and baptismal font. Behind the altar was a gilded triptych. Or maybe it wasn't gilt, but actual gold. Each of its three panels rose to a point topped with a small cross, looking much like a replica of the church itself. A much larger cross rose above the triptych. Shining down on the altar were a half-circle of stained-glass windows rising to the domed roof of the cupola.

But what drew my eyes was two chairs pushed against the wall to the right of the altar. They had unusually tall backs, carved much like the triptych with small crosses on top, and were undoubtedly intended for church dignitaries. But I ran down the aisle and climbed onto the closest. Closing my eyes, I pretended with all the determination of my small heart and mind that I'd just climbed into my heavenly daddy's lap, the God who had created this beautiful world and indwelt this church. I began telling him all about school and the Russian soldiers on the road and my trips across the Czech border. I thanked him for keeping me safe from the bombs and soldiers and border patrols. As I talked, I leaned back against the chair, pretending that my invisible Friend had his two arms around my waist, as any father might cradle a beloved child.

That was the third turning-point of my life. You may remember, reader, that the first was on the basement steps the day the first bomb fell, when I aged sixty years in just sixty seconds. The second was on Christmas night when that invisible Presence warned me not to enter the first cave. And the third was when I sat on God's lap in that church.

Maybe you are thinking it was just a child's silly make-believe. But I can tell you, dear reader, as clearly as I live and breathe today that at that moment I felt God's tender arms around me. For the first time in my life, I felt completely secure, accepted, and loved. I stopped talking and just let the quiet peace of that church sanctuary seep into me. I still remember my thoughts. *It's okay if I don't have people to love me, because I am loved by Someone wonderful, even if I can't see him.*

And suddenly at that moment, just as when I'd last been in a church as a four-year-old flower girl, I felt overwhelmed by a sense of holiness. It made me feel nervous, but at the same time I didn't want to ever leave this place. Of course, I knew I had to leave eventually. Already, Lisbeth would be angry that I was late. So at last, I slipped down from the chair and headed back down the aisle. When I reached the entrance, I started to open the heavy double doors. But instead, I turned around for one last look at God's beautiful house and the chair where I had been sitting on his lap.

Remember what happened here today, I told myself. *Any time in the future when you feel rejected, lonely, and abandoned, just remember this moment. You are not an abandoned, unloved child anymore. You are the daughter of a heavenly Vater who loves you very much.*

Then I stepped outside, closed the doors behind me, and began the long walk home. The tall, pine woods had never seemed so beautiful, and the sense of God's presence went with me. From then on, even on those scary nights when I was racing over the border, I no longer felt alone. I would just let my mind go back to that church and chair and the wonderful, comforting sensation of sitting on God's lap.

Years later, I would discover that I was not the only person to have such an experience with God when I read for the first time this beautiful psalm written by King David:

> My heart is not proud, Lord, my eyes are not haughty; I do not concern myself with great matters or things too wonderful for me. But I have calmed and quieted myself, *I am like a weaned child with its mother,* like a weaned child I am content. Israel, put your hope in the Lord both now and forevermore.
>
> —Psalm 131

CHAPTER THIRTEEN

SHIPBOARD

Have I not commanded you? Be strong and
courageous. Do not be afraid; do not be
discouraged, for the Lord your God will be with you
wherever you go.

—Joshua 1:9

I could never have guessed that day in the church
sanctuary that my time in Bad Elster was drawing swiftly
to its end. In fact, I would not see *St. Trinitatis Kirche*
again or walk through those beautiful woods for another forty
years.

What precipitated this new upheaval in my life was my
thirteenth birthday. By this point, the Soviet Union's grip on
eastern Germany was complete. Its citizens would live under
one more totalitarian regime for another forty years. But I
was not just a German citizen, though I thought little since
leaving Plauen about that American birth certificate.
Unfortunately, by German law, my dual citizenship would
end when I turned fourteen. If I was still in Germany on
November 7, 1948, I would forfeit my American citizenship.

Which in turn meant that I would be locked permanently inside the Russian sector.

If I knew none of this at the time, it was clearly of some concern to my aunt Lisbeth and my birth mother, who had remained in sporadic contact with each other since the end of the war. Despite my mother's abandonment of me and all that would happen later, I am thankful to look back and know that at least on this one occasion my mother cared enough to exert herself on my behalf. This included a trip to Washington, D. C. to explain how her American-born daughter had ended up in east Germany and to apply for my exit visa from Germany.

Meanwhile, Lisbeth made contact with the American consulate in West Berlin, where she had to show my birth certificate to prove I was an American. My mother sent money for ship passage, a passport, and other paperwork. I was twelve years old when they started the process, but it took so long and involved so many back and forth trips that I was thirteen and a half years old by the time my passport and exit visa arrived.

I packed my few belongings in a wooden suitcase. Then Lisbeth and I traveled to Plauen so that I could say goodbye to all my extended family and friends there. This proved so emotionally painful that I stopped telling people I was leaving Germany for good. Instead, I told my friends I was just visiting from Bad Elster and wanted to say hello. My best friend Maria had moved from Plauen, so I didn't get to say goodbye to her. But I did visit Frau Benner, to whom I poured out my real story and how sad I was to say goodbye.

"Well, Eleanor, you are a strong person with a lot of potential," Frau Benner consoled, putting her arms around me and hugging me tight. "You will be a strong woman someday. And things will be easier for you now because you will be with your mother."

She'd surmised correctly that much of my fears and insecurity stemmed from not having a mother. I didn't tell her that I was not, in fact, going to a mother who had ever loved or wanted me. That was my most difficult parting. Lisbeth and I then boarded the train to Berlin. At this time, Berlin was divided into sectors just like Germany itself, but the infamous Berlin Wall had not yet been built. So Berlin was actually a crossing point, both legally and illegally, for many Germans into West Germany.

Because Lisbeth was East German, she couldn't cross over into western Berlin, much less into West Germany. My planned itinerary was to fly from West Berlin over the Russian zone to the coast, where I would board a ship to the United States. But when we arrived, not all our paperwork was ready. The American consulate made arrangements for us to stay in the home of a war widow, who ran it as a boarding house for people waiting for passage to the United States. We ended up staying there for several weeks.

Also waiting for passage was another teenage girl, several years older than me, and her mother. During our wait, we received regular care packages from the American consulate, including chocolate, tea, packaged cookies, and other goodies. Every afternoon, the other girl would go down to the street, then bring up a soldier and retreat into her bedroom with him. Sometime later, she would emerge with the soldier and prepare afternoon tea for him in the kitchen from our care packages. Once again, I was too naïve to realize until much later that she was a prostitute.

Finally, my paperwork arrived. Lisbeth and I were driven to the airport along with the other girl and her mother. Since Lisbeth couldn't leave the Russian sector, this would be our final goodbye, perhaps forever. I had already made up my mind that I would not cry. I knew that if I allowed myself to feel emotion, I would never get on that plane. I would just stay behind, become a German citizen, and forget all this America stuff.

Still, Lisbeth was the only mother I had known since I was two years old. Except for those days on the farm, I had never been apart from her a single night in my memory. So I could not stifle a sharp pang of hurt when Lisbeth didn't even give me a goodbye hug, but just turned away. Maybe like me, she didn't dare show emotion lest she begin crying or change her mind about letting me go. At least I could hope that was the reason, rather than that the woman who'd played the role of my mother for the past eleven years just couldn't get rid of me fast enough.

Turning, I followed the other passengers up a movable staircase into the plane. I didn't look back or wave. I was on my way to a new mother, a new father, and a new country whose language I didn't even know. Being on a plane was a new experience for me as well, and I watched with fascination as the ground fell away below us, the buildings and cars and roads quickly shrinking to the size of toys. A stewardess handed out gum. Chewing was supposed to help equalize air pressure in our ears as the plane reached cruising altitude. I didn't know that, so I swallowed the gum, thinking it was candy.

I didn't know it then, but I was very fortunate I left when I did. Just one month after my departure, the Russians cut off access from West Germany to the Allied sectors of Berlin. The ensuing blockade would lead to the Berlin Airlift, the largest air relief operation in human history, under the auspices of American president Harry Truman, supplying food and fuel for two million west Berliners through the winter of 1948-1949. By the time the Russians lifted the blockade in May, 1949, I would have been fourteen years old, so I might never have reached America if I'd left even one month later.

Our flight from Berlin to Bremerhaven took less than an hour. Bremerhaven is the seaport for the city of Bremen on the North Sea. During WWII, it was the top Nazi navy base, but it was now a major Allied shipping center. Lisbeth had told me someone from the Red Cross would be waiting to look after me. But no one showed up or asked for me. Instead, I was informed that my paperwork for the ship had not yet arrived, and I was taken to a military barracks.

The barracks held at least a hundred other people who were also waiting for their paperwork, but I was easily the youngest person there. I stayed there several more weeks, which proved quite an education, since men and women were sharing the barracks, and this time I could see in living color what was going on in the bunks around me. Pulling the covers over my head, I prayed, *Okay, God, you kept me safe from bombs, so you can keep a man out of my bed.* Then I went to sleep without any fear. Sure enough, I was not touched during my time there.

At thirteen, I considered myself quite adult, and I was not shy at all. Staying all day in the barracks with nothing to do was excruciatingly boring. One day I read a request posted by a local resident on the communal bulletin board for someone to do ironing. I went to the barracks guard and asked if I could go to the woman's house and offer my services.

"So long as you make sure you come back," he responded.

I left the barracks and started walking until I found the address indicated. There I introduced myself to the woman. "Hi, my name is Eleanor. I saw your note, and I'd be happy to come and iron for you."

The woman served me tea and asked me about myself and what I was doing in the barracks. After telling her my story, I started ironing. When I finished, she gave me some money. I'd thought this was just a volunteer chore and hadn't expected to be paid, so I was thrilled. Stopping at a store on the way back to the barracks, I used the money to buy a bottle of clear fingernail polish. As I painted my fingernails, I felt truly grownup.

There was little else to do in the barracks. But each week, we would all be called to a big meeting where the names of those whose papers had arrived would be called out. It was quite a while before mine was called, but it turned out we had to wait for the ship anyway, so it didn't really matter. By the time the ship arrived, everyone in the barracks had their papers.

The ship was called the S. S. Marine Flasher, and it was actually an American troop transport, which had been repurposed after the war to carry emigrants from Europe to the United States. From 1946-1949, it sailed back and forth from Bremerhaven to Ellis Island, carrying nine hundred refugees on each trip, including many Jewish concentration camp survivors. What I remember most of our departure was hundreds of people hanging over the deck railing to wave goodbye to their family members and friends, who were all crowded along the shore, waving back.

I had no one to wave goodbye to, so I headed below deck to my assigned bunk, which was near the boiler room. Once again, I addressed my invisible Friend. *I don't need anyone to wave goodbye to me, because I have You. And You aren't leaving me alone. You're coming with me on my trip, so I'll be just fine.*

And that is how I dealt with the rest of my trans-Atlantic voyage. Every time I'd feel a twinge of pain and loneliness, I would retreat immediately in my mind to my secret place. There, I would find something positive to think about instead of the fact that I was even more alone than I'd ever been until now. You know, that is actually a wonderful way to live. To this day, I always try to stay positive, no matter how sad, lonely, and unpredictable things might be. I have faith that even if it doesn't look possible now, things will turn out alright in the end.

My dearest reader, if you take nothing else away from this book (and I hope you will take away many things!), may I encourage you to take away this advice. When things get tough, look for the silver lining. Nature itself teaches us that principle. No matter how dark and stormy the sky, we know that up above the clouds, the sun is always shining. Keep that in mind, and you will get through the tough times. Sooner or later, the sun will come out, and things will get better.

My first real joy on that ship was going to breakfast. At first I just stood there, stunned. I'd never seen a table with so much food—eggs, ham, toast, jelly, muffins. Instead of coffee, there was all the milk you wanted to drink. In Bad

Elster, our egg ration had been one a year. That morning, when I finished my first two eggs, the waiter brought two more, then two more. After six eggs, I finally shook my head to another helping.

Every meal during that trip, I was the last person out of the dining-room. The waiters got a real kick out of my ferocious appetite. With a big smile, they'd just keep piling more food on my plate, and I'd keep eating. I in turn could not remember the last time I'd been able to eat until I was completely full. They also gave me my first Coca Cola. It was in a glass bottle and icy-cold. They let me take the bottle up on deck. I stood at the railing, sipping at the sweet, dark liquid through a long, plastic straw. Maybe going to America wouldn't be so bad!

CHAPTER FOURTEEN

AMERICA

Though my father and mother forsake me, the LORD
will receive me.

—Psalm 27:10

In all, the trip lasted two weeks. The S. S. Marine
Flasher arrived in New York Harbor at 5 p.m. on
Wednesday, May 26, 1948. Significantly, though I had no
idea at the time, this means that I was at sea on May 14,
1948, when Israel declared its independence and became a
nation again for the first time in almost two thousand years.
As the ship slowed to enter the dock, I was leaning over the
deck rail, eager to see this new country, when I felt a touch
on my shoulder.

"Eleanor, do you see that statue over there?"

I turned to see one of the female passengers. Since I was
the only child on board, everyone knew me by name. She
went on, "That's called the Statue of Liberty. Do you know
what it means?"

When I shook my head, she explained, "It means you are
free. Now that you are in America, you don't ever have to be

hungry anymore. You don't have to run from bombs. You can be anything you want—a teacher, lawyer, doctor. You can take out a loan, go to school, graduate, get a job, and pay it back. This country is a wonderful place to live."

Then she walked away. I was left there, staring at the gigantic, green statue of a woman with a crown on her head that rose from an island in the middle of the harbor. As the ship eased into dock, I retreated to my secret place and began to talk to my invisible Friend. I guess I could call it prayer, though I didn't yet know that word. I still remember the words I spoke.

God, we have to talk. This is a whole, new life for me, and I know it is going to be wonderful. You got me through some very hard times during the war. Here in America, it will probably be a lot easier for you to take care of me. But you will have to help me learn their language and learn to know my mother. You know I can't go back, so I have to make a life for myself in America and be happy here. I have no other choice. So please help me do all that.

Picking up my wooden suitcase, I headed for the gangplank. I was the fifth person off the ship. Most of the passengers were being herded onto ferries to be shuttled over to Ellis Island, the island I'd seen where the Statue of Liberty stood. At that time, it was also the center where immigrants were processed to enter the United States. Since I was an American citizen, I didn't have to go through immigration. Instead, I presented my passport to a Customs official, who slammed down a stamp right under my photograph.

I still have that passport today. The black-and-white photograph shows my thirteen-year-old self looking pensive under a mass of dark curls cut just above my shoulders. My full name—Eleanor Elsie Drechsler—is signed down one side of the photo in my schoolgirl cursive. Below the photo in smeared blue ink is my entry stamp, a round seal lettered around its border "DEPARTMENT OF JUSTICE IMMG. & NATZN. SERVICE". In the center are the words "Admitted May 26, 1948, New York, N. Y."

At long last, I was back in the country of my birth. I looked around, trying to spot my mother, though I wasn't sure what she looked like. In fact, both my parents had come to meet me. They hadn't seen me since I was a toddler, so they had no idea what I looked like either. I learned afterwards that a nearby woman had said to my mother, "Look, there's a little girl getting off the ship. She looks just like you."

"Yes, that's my daughter," my mother responded. "I'm waiting to pick her up."

Taking my mother by the hand, the woman had walked her over to me. That was how I met Mom, as I learned to call her American-style, for the first time in my memory. She was a very pretty, elegant woman. A moment later, my father, or Pop, arrived, along with my great-aunt Klara, my grandmother Minna's sister, who had been the one to originally sponsor my parents when they came to the United States.

Pop was a tall, good-looking man. But he looked angry, and I was instantly afraid of him. I knew my parents were divorced, and their dislike for each other was evident. I remember thinking to myself, *Uh, oh, I've just finished one war, and I'm not going to get into another one with these people!*

"Hello," Mom greeted me with a nervous smile. She made no attempt to hug me, nor did my father. Since I'd never been hugged by anyone but Frau Benner, that didn't bother me. These people were total strangers to me, so I didn't know how to react. But I followed as Pop picked up my wooden suitcase and led the way to his car.

I was ushered into the front seat between my father, who was driving, and my mother. Mom was at least smiling, but Pop still looked angry. Squeezed between them, I was so nervous I just started chattering. I talked about the ship and having all the eggs I could eat and anything else I could think of for the entire ninety-minute trip from New York Harbor to Union, NJ, where my mother had an apartment.

Mom's apartment was upstairs in a house belonging to a woman I learned quickly to call Tante Emmy, though she was not actually my aunt. Tante Emmy wrote poetry and was immediately kind to me. When we walked up the front steps, she opened the door, gave me a big hug, then picked me up and carried me over the threshold. At thirteen, I found this a little embarrassing. But it was far more a welcome than I'd received from my parents.

She accompanied us upstairs into the apartment. I was stunned and overwhelmed to see the whole place decorated for a party. Crepe banners hung from the ceiling. Presents were scattered around the living-room. Then people began pouring in. This was the German neighborhood of Union, so I had no problem understanding them. But it took a while for me to realize that this was a welcome home party for me.

I was ushered to a seat and began opening the presents. Among the gifts was a Bulova watch, something I'd never dreamed of possessing. Other packages held a blouse, nightgown, chocolate, and a pair of slip-on loafers. One woman handed me two dollars and a banana. I had no idea what a banana was, so I just held it awkwardly.

"It's a piece of fruit," the woman explained. "You can eat it."

I obediently bit into the banana, which tasted bitter and oily. The woman shook her head. "No, no! You have to take off the skin."

Once peeled, the banana tasted better, though quite dry compared to apples, peaches, or other fruit I'd eaten. In all this time, my father had not once spoken to me. By the time the neighbors all left, he'd gone too, leaving Mom and me alone in the apartment. That was when she started talking. She told me all about her divorce, what a horrible person Pop was, how she'd had to get a job in a factory to survive, how difficult and unfair things were for her.

Not once did Mom ask me a single question about my own life. She certainly knew from her communications with Lisbeth that we'd survived bombings and starvation and all the trauma of war, but she acted as though there'd never even been a war. Nor did she ever offer an explanation for why she'd abandoned me in Germany to begin with or why she'd left me there during all the horrors of WWII. I might have been returning from a brief, pleasurable vacation abroad instead of eleven years of abandonment and exile.

In the beginning, Mom was at least smiling, showing me around the apartment, presenting me with a nicely-appointed bedroom, much as though I were some visiting acquaintance, instead of her long-lost daughter. An adult acquaintance at that, since soon she was telling me all about her sex life. But by the third day, she'd let down her guard and began reminiscing about how angry she'd been when she found out she was pregnant with me. She laughed over how she'd tried to trigger a miscarriage by pushing around her heavy refrigerator. She told me how furious my father had been when I was born a girl instead of the son he wanted. She'd thrown out any pictures of me. In fact, the few pictures I have today of my pre-Germany childhood are ones that had been sent to my grandparents, who eventually gave them to me.

In all this, Mom laughed and smiled as though sharing funny anecdotes with a new friend. It never seemed to occur to her that such reminiscences could be deeply painful to the daughter she hadn't wanted. I'd arrived on a Wednesday. For three days, I listened and listened and listened. By Saturday, I realized two things. One, I was more grownup than this woman who had given birth to me. All she did was talk and brag about herself like a little girl. Two, I hadn't had a mother in Germany, and I still didn't have one.

Okay, God, so I still don't have a mother, I spoke heavenward as I listened to Mom's prattling. *I'm clearly not meant to ever have a mother. So I guess it is you and me. You are my father and mother.*

Years later, I found a Bible verse that has always remained a sweet promise to me. It is in another of the psalms written by King David, who knew well what it was to be rejected, abandoned, and lonely in those long years of exile and hiding before God made him king of Israel.

> Though my father and mother forsake me, the Lord will receive me. I remain confident of this: I will see the goodness of the Lord in the land of the living. Wait for the Lord; be strong and take heart and wait for the Lord.

—Psalm 27:10, 13-14

I'd vowed to make a good life for myself in this new land where I was living. If my father and mother didn't want me here, I would cling to the one Person I knew did care about me enough to save me repeatedly from certain death. He'd given me assurance that I would not only survive, but grow up to know him and have a full, abundant life in a place of peace and beauty. I would just have to wait patiently a while longer than I'd anticipated.

Meanwhile, I didn't dare tell Mom how I really felt. She'd sent me away once, and I was afraid that if I angered her, she might send me back to Germany. So I decided the best thing I could do was to become her best friend so she'd want to keep me around. I'd become an expert at pretending and hiding my own feelings over the last few years. So I pretended she was a stranger—which, in fact, she was!—who was allowing me to stay with her.

I laughed and smiled at her stories. I pitched in to cook, clean, and wash dishes. I behaved as sweetly, kindly, and compliantly as I could. And I kept my own mouth shut. The eleven years of abandonment, rejection, loneliness, and trauma were swept under the carpet as though they'd never been.

That became our relationship for many decades to come. Mom never did change. Years later, when I was routinely being asked to speak about my WWII experiences, Mom refused to attend any of my speaking engagements. In fact, to the day she died, she had no idea of the events I've told you about in this book. When I was at any public event or social engagement, it wasn't uncommon for someone to ask,

"Eleanor, you went through the war. You lived under Hitler. What was it like for you?"

If Mom was with me, she'd immediately interrupt with a laugh, "Oh, it was not so bad for Eleanor! She did just fine."

Then she'd promptly and firmly change the subject to what a good pot roast we were eating or the weather or any other subject but the war. Whether or not she wanted to admit it, I came to understand that she did this because she felt guilty. By then, I'd learned what God had to say about getting back at those who hurt you:

> Do not repay anyone evil for evil . . . If it is possible, as far as it depends on you, live at peace with everyone . . . for it is written: "It is mine to avenge; I will repay," says the Lord.
>
> —Romans 12:17-19; Deuteronomy 32:35

I could not change my mother, and she made abundantly clear she had no intention of changing herself. But I could choose to love her or not love her. To live in peace or conflict. In the end, I chose to let it go and leave Mom in God's hands.

CHAPTER FIFTEEN

UNWANTED

Know that the LORD is God. It is he who made us,
and we are his; we are his people . . .

—Psalm 100:3

I'd arrived in New Jersey in late May, so the school year
had not yet ended. During that interminable first
weekend, I told Mom I wanted to go to school on Monday
like every other child. She agreed and took me in to the local
school before heading to work. One complication
immediately arose, which was that I hardly spoke a word of
English. We went first to the principal's office to fill out
necessary paperwork. When the principal asked me for my
address. I thought he was referencing my dress, so I
answered, "Blue."

Another awkward moment arose when the principal asked
Mom what grade I was in. Since she'd bothered to learn
nothing about me, she had to ask me what grade I was in,
which must have puzzled the principal. Once we translated
the German system into its American equivalent, they
decided that I was just finishing seventh grade. Since I knew

no English, the principal decided to have me repeat seventh grade the following year.

Meanwhile, I was walked down the hall to a classroom. The students all looked so strange to me, so young and confident, while I had felt like an old woman since the first bomb attack. My German clothing was somber and dark compared to the frilly pastels and full skirts of the other girls. The class was studying geography, and as I took my seat, the teacher said something about Illinois. I thought she was saying my name, Eleanor, and welcoming me to the class.

Determined to stay positive, I reminded my invisible Friend, *Okay, I said you'd have to help me learn English. And no one else is helping, so it is up to you to help me do this!*

I decided to start my own dictionary. Every time I could make out a distinct word in English, I wrote it down phonetically in German. When I got home, I asked Mom or Tante Emmy what each word meant. This proved confusing as well, since words that sounded exactly the same turned out to be spelled differently and have completely different meanings, like sail and sale, their, there, and they're, would and wood. The school year ended two weeks later, but I continued my dictionary, determined to acquire a reasonable fluency in English by the time school started again in the fall. I collected English words and phrases doggedly, practicing them with the landlady, neighbors, store clerks, and anyone else I could find.

I also found a job babysitting for a neighbor. It felt wonderful to have some pocket money of my own. Later in the summer, I found a job helping in a vegetable stand as well. By this time, Mom had taken me shopping to buy some more American-looking clothing, so I no longer stood out as a foreigner. That is, until I opened my mouth. I still remember offering a bunch of carrots to my very first customer: *"Halo? Ein Boonch kaa-rots?"*

The vegetable stand owner was very understanding and kind. She helped me learn English and taught me new words for my dictionary. On top of my wages, she'd give me an extra tip and send me home with leftover vegetables. If I received no love at home, I am grateful there have always been some nice people in my life—Maria and her mother, Frau Benner, Tante Emmy, the vegetable stand owner—to show me kindness and affection. That would continue to be the case in years to come.

By now, I'd seen Pop several times. He lived in New York, but every other Saturday, he drove to New Jersey to pick me up for a visit. From those visits, I learned a bit about Pop's life. Both my parents had become American citizens, and like every other able-bodied American male, Pop had fought in WWII, though in the Pacific theater against Japan. Unlike his brothers, who'd fought for Germany, he'd made it through the war unscathed, at least physically. He was no longer a baker, but worked in a factory. He was also remarried to a young woman named Billie.

One Saturday, Pop and Billie decided to take me to see the Statue of Liberty and other New York sights. They also bought me a pretty dress. My father behaved pleasantly, and I was not unhappy to be getting to know him a little better. Unfortunately, when Pop and Billie dropped me back off in front of my mother's apartment, Mom was looking out a window. Billie gave me a hug as I climbed out of the car. That was enough to set Mom off into a screaming, crying fit of hysteria.

The gist of her ranting included, "How dare he bring that woman here! They are trying to steal you away from me. They are going to take you away and never bring you back."

Even after Pop and Billie left, Mom kept screaming. I didn't know what to do. I might have thought she cared so much about me that she was jealous of any attention I received from Pop. But her rantings made clear she was far more angry about Pop's new wife showing up at her house. I finally managed to calm her down, but inside I was thinking, *God, I can't take all this screaming. I said I wouldn't get involved in another war. Not after finally escaping the last one.*

The next time Pop came to pick me up, Billie was once again with him. Instead of coming upstairs, Pop whistled loudly so I'd know to come down. Before I could respond, Mom was already screaming hysterically. I could think of only one course of action. It might not have been the wisest one, but I was only a thirteen-year-old girl, and it felt like I was having to be the grown-up referee between two quarrelling toddlers.

I went down to Pop's car, but I didn't climb in. Instead, I told my father, "Look, as you can see, Mom gets very upset when you pick me up. She thinks you're going to steal me away and not bring me back. So would you mind if we just give it a few weeks before you come back? Let me settle in, and let Mom get used to the idea. Then we can try again."

Pop said nothing, his expression furious. But Billie spoke up quickly. "Okay, maybe we'll come back in July."

They drove off, but they never did come back. Mom expressed great glee that I'd sent them away. I didn't feel any real sadness, since Pop and Billie were basically strangers. My only real thought had been to uncomplicate my life since it was Mom I had to live with day in and day out. Still, I was disappointed and puzzled that my father hadn't returned for another visit.

Later that year, I made a point of taking some of my babysitting money and purchasing a pen and pencil set. I'd found out the date of Pop's birthday, and I still had his mailing address. So I wrote out a birthday card to my father, then mailed the pen and pencil set to him as a birthday present. A week later, the package came back with a note from my father that read, "I don't need your pen and pencil set!"

This deeply hurt me. He'd done nothing when Mom gave me away the first time. Now it was as though he was simply tossing me away once more. And sure enough, that was the last time Pop ever contacted me, and it would be many years before I saw him again. Nor did I hear from Lisbeth. In coming years, my premonition proved true. Once a year around the holidays, we'd call Germany to speak to various relatives. But Lisbeth herself never bothered contacting me other than the occasional Christmas card.

Retreating to my inner secret place, I reminded myself over and over, *Whatever these people do, it doesn't matter, because they are not my father and mother. I have no father and mother, and I never did. But that's okay. God is my father and mother, and that's all that matters.*

In September, I started seventh grade. I was relieved to discover that my dictionary and all my hard work studying English had paid off. I was able to understand my teachers and had no difficulties keeping up with the homework. But just a few weeks later, I left that school. During all these months, one thing I haven't mentioned is that my mother had a boyfriend. His name was Otto Steimle, and he too was German, an immigrant from Bavaria. He was a factory foreman and, unlike my mother, had never been married before.

In October, Mom and Otto were married, and we moved to a new house near his factory job, but a half-hour drive from Tante Emmy's house, in a town called Kenilworth. I didn't mind the move. The house was of brand-new construction and much nicer than the apartment. I was even allowed to pick the wallpaper for my bedroom. I'd made no friends at the first school, so I was fine with moving to a new one.

But in other ways, I was struggling with life in America, especially since I had no one to explain things to me. After our move, Mom found a new factory job. It wasn't at the factory where Otto was foreman, but another neighbor worked with her, so Mom carpooled with the neighbor, leaving the house at 7 a.m. and getting home after 5 p.m.

This wasn't new to me, since Lisbeth had always worked as well. But along with school, I was also now in charge of making meals and keeping the house clean. I didn't have to do the shopping, as there was a grocery store that made deliveries. I would call in once or twice a week, ordering potatoes, steak, butter, fish, jelly, and other groceries. I had never cooked before, but I would watch Mom cook a dish once, then duplicate it.

Once again, I found myself very much alone. Going to school, doing homework, and keeping house were my only activities. When Mom was home, she remained harsh and uncaring. One pleasure I'd discovered on my voyage to America was eating. Before then, scarcity of food had kept me thin. With all the food I wanted, I'd gained a fair amount of weight on the trip over. Not that I was fat, but the picture of my arrival in New York shows a chubby-cheeked young teen. Now I started eating to relieve my loneliness. I was soon a size twelve, then fourteen. My mother mocked me for this.

"If you ever get a boyfriend," she told me, "he is going to fall in love with me because I'm a lot prettier than you are."

Looking back, I cannot believe any mother would say that to their vulnerable fourteen-year-old daughter. But then, she never treated me as a daughter, rather as another female invading the queen bee's territory. Her taunting rang in my ears for years, making me feel constantly self-conscious about my looks and weight. So much that I was thirty years old before I dared accept a young man purchasing me a chocolate sundae or any other fattening treat. I accepted that I was too ugly and fat for any boy to like me. In any case, I wasn't really interested in dating. The truth was that I'd always been rather afraid of men, since I'd grown up almost entirely in female company. None of my experiences with Lisbeth's boyfriends and husband, my stepfather, or my own father ameliorated my unease in male company.

In fact, though my English was now fluent, and I dressed like any other American teen, I didn't feel that I fit in with my classmates. I was a very old person emotionally, and they all seemed so young and carefree. While I thought of bombs and starvation and worried about another global war, the other girls talked only about boys, dresses, makeup, or their favorite movies. It was easier to go home, cook or do my schoolwork, and think deep thoughts about life. I felt as though I'd failed at making a good, new life for myself in America, and that troubled me. I hadn't forgotten my vow that if I survived the war, I would seek out my invisible Friend and find out what his purpose was for sparing my life. At least I now knew his name.

God, when you first became my Friend, I was running for my life with absolutely nothing! I prayed. *Now I have everything I could ever want. But my life feels so empty. Why did you bother saving me? What is the purpose of it all?*

Finding the truth about my invisible Friend became my quest. By this time, I'd had my first real exposure to religion, specifically, to Christianity, though what I'd picked up was very much a jumble of disconnected information. It might seem odd today that school was where I learned such things. But at that time, prayer and Scripture had not yet been banished from America's public schools. Our homeroom teacher read a passage from the Bible every morning. At first, I didn't know what book she was reading, but all the students became quiet and respectful when she read, and the words were beautiful, so I enjoyed it. I also remember having to memorize Psalm 100:

> Make a joyful noise unto the Lord, all ye lands. Serve the Lord with gladness: come before his presence with singing. Know ye that the Lord he is God: it is he that hath made us, and not we ourselves; we are his people, and the sheep of his pasture. Enter into his gates with thanksgiving, and into his courts with praise: be thankful unto him, and bless his name. For the Lord is good; his mercy is everlasting; and his truth endureth to all generations (KJV).

All of this confirmed to me that my invisible Friend was indeed the God who'd created me and who could be found in church buildings like the one in Bad Elster. I'd also learned who Jesus was. While I did not fit in with American teenagers, teachers liked me because I was polite, quiet, and studied hard. They also discovered that I had a good singing voice, and I was invited to sing in the school choir. Unlike in Germany under the Nazis and Russians, American Yuletide carols were often about a Jewish carpenter named Jesus. In fact, to my surprise, it turned out that the school Yuletide program actually celebrated the birth of this Jewish carpenter.

How Jesus related to the Creator of this universe or why people were still singing about him after two thousand years, I had not yet pieced together. Keep in mind that none of my family or teachers in Germany, nor my mother and stepfather here in America ever spoke about God, religion, and definitely not about Jesus.

PICTURES

Eleanor Isaacson, age two, before being taken to Germany.

Eleanor with her parents, Arthur and Hilda Drechsler, before being taken to Germany.

Eleanor's paternal grandparents, Otto and Minna Drechsler, with children. Eleanor's father Arthur is standing at extreme left.

Opa (grandfather) Otto Drechsler outside
his bakery in Plauen.

Eleanor's maternal grandparents, Elsa
and Paul Handel, with children.
Eleanor's mother Hilda is at the far left.

Eleanor, age three, enjoying Sunday outing with aunt Lisbeth and her husband Walter.

Eleanor, age four, with new doll carriage.

Eleanor, age four, as flower girl in a
wedding.

Eleanor and younger cousin Ruth.

Cave where Eleanor and other Plauen residents sheltered from bomb attacks.

Interior of second cave shelter Eleanor
felt led to hide.

Bomb destruction in Plauen after Allied attacks.

Plauen after the bombings.

Looking down on destroyed Plauen with single surviving church that rang bells signaling end of war.

Tree that became makeshift post office
and relocation center after war ended.

Border police housing where Eleanor
lived under Russian occupation.

East Germany-Czechoslovakian border
point where Eleanor crossed as a child
smuggler.

Lutheran Church of the Holy Trinity where Eleanor encountered God as her heavenly Father.

Interior of Lutheran Church of the Holy Trinity. Note the ceremonial chairs on the right where, as a child, Eleanor "sat on her heavenly daddy's lap."

Passport entry from Eleanor's return to America in 1948.

Bob and Eleanor Isaacson's wedding
photo.

The New Jersey home Bob and Eleanor
designed together.

Backyard garden of Bob and Eleanor's
New Jersey home.

Portrait of Dr. Robert and Eleanor
Isaacson.

Eleanor visiting a rebuilt Plauen.

Eleanor winning first place at NYC
ballroom dance competition.

Eleanor and mother Hilda at Hilda's 90th birthday party.

Eleanor in her red BMW convertible (AT LAST!) enjoying being young with young friends. Dear Reader, this is proof that God restores the years that the locusts consume (Joel 2:25).

Living a rich, full, vibrant widowhood at age 82.

CHAPTER SIXTEEN

SEARCHING

For God did not send his Son into the world to condemn the world, but to save the world through him.

—John 3:16

I n 1950, I started high school, so I now had to take a bus to get to school. I made one good friend there named Betty who was of a German family. By now I was routinely being invited to sing solos, and she was my accompanist on the piano. We spent a lot of time practicing together in the auditorium during our study halls. Like me, she was of German parentage, though she spoke only English. By this point, I was speaking only English as well even at home. I'd acquired an American accent well enough that no one knew I'd grown up in Germany unless someone told them.

But I had not forgotten my quest. Nor had I forgotten how close to God I'd felt in that Bad Elster church. One day, I stopped by a Methodist church that was walking distance from my house, where I made an appointment to speak to the pastor. I asked him how I could get close to God.

"I want to connect with God," I explained. "But I don't know where to find him. What should I do?"

"You need to join the church and teach Sunday school," the pastor told me.

We talked for a long time. Night had fallen by the time I left. The moon was full, the streets empty of people and cars. Looking up at that full moon, I prayed, *Okay, God, you know how much I want to connect with you. Perhaps now I will.*

I began attending that church. I sang in its choir. I taught a children's Sunday school class. This just entailed reading the Sunday school manual and repeating it to the children. But since I had no real understanding of what I was reading, I became even more confused. That the pastor would give me a Sunday school class when I knew nothing about God, Christianity, or the Bible is a good indication of how shallow their teaching was. The Sunday morning liturgy had not helped me connect with God, and eventually I stopped attending.

But I hadn't given up my quest. One thing that had become clear, both from church and the school Christmas programs, was a connection between the Jewish carpenter, Jesus, and God. One Saturday when I was off school and Mom was off work, Mom took me to the Atlantic City boardwalk. This was a famous New Jersey tourist attraction right on the ocean with amusement rides, shopping, casinos, and public beaches for swimming, surfing, and sailing. One of the shop windows displayed religious paraphernalia, including statuettes and wall pictures of Jesus, the Virgin Mary, and other saints.

Since I'd heard so much about Jesus since coming to America, I decided to buy one of the statuettes, its Italianate shoulder-length hair, features, and beard purporting to be a depiction of Jesus. Maybe it would help me feel closer to God. Taking it home, I set it up in a prominent spot in my room like a little shrine. I also began reading books about religion—not just Christianity, but Buddhism and various eastern mystic cults.

But none of this gave me any sense of connection with my invisible Friend. It occurred to me I was going about this all wrong. That Atlantic City shop wasn't selling its religious icons just for decoration. One day after school, I retreated to my room, faced the statuette of Jesus, and bowed down towards it.

Okay, are you God? I addressed the statuette. *How can I find out about you?*

I neither heard nor felt a response, not even the quiet inner communication I'd known in the past from my invisible Friend. I picked up the statuette and turned it over. Stamped on the bottom was its place of manufacture. I don't remember where that was, but it suddenly occurred to me that if this statue was made in a factory, why was I bowing down and praying to it? How could something formed by human hands have anything to do with an invisible, eternal God?

In a fury of revulsion, I wrapped the statue in paper so I could not see it anymore, then threw it in the trash. Nervously, I hoped I hadn't done something wrong in disposing of the image. Years later, I found my answer in the words of the Old Testament prophet Jeremiah:

The practices of the peoples are worthless; they cut
a tree out of the forest, and a craftsman shapes it
with his chisel. They adorn it with silver and gold;
they fasten it with hammer and nails so it will not
totter. Like a scarecrow in a cucumber field, their
idols cannot speak; they must be carried because
they cannot walk. Do not fear them; they can do no
harm nor can they do any good . . . *But the Lord is
the true God; he is the living God, the eternal King.*

—Jeremiah 10:3-5, 10

While I recognized that the statuette was just plaster,
paint, and gilt, I was still no closer to finding the true, living
God. I longed for the feeling of closeness to my heavenly
daddy I'd experienced sitting on God's lap in the Bad Elster
cathedral. Had I just imagined it all?

In desperation, I hopped on a bus one Saturday and rode
it into Cranford, NJ, about two miles from Kenilworth, where
I'd seen a beautiful Catholic church. Just as in Bad Elster, I
found the doors unlocked and the sanctuary empty. The
marbled floor was cool beneath my feet, the steeply-arched
ceiling high above my head, as I walked down the long aisle
to a penitent rail. Beyond it, steps led up to the altar. Here
there were no stained-glass windows, but a full-sized cross
on the wall behind the altar. A tortured figure of Jesus,
complete with thorny crown and red streaks for the blood,
was nailed to it.

Kneeling on the padded rise intended for penitents, I
stared up at the life-sized crucifix. Could this person who
hung dead and abandoned on that cross help me find God?
I knelt there for a long time, staring up at the figure of Jesus.

Then something twisted in my heart. That painted decoration up on the church wall was no less man-made, if more unpleasant to look at, than the mass-produced statuette I'd purchased in Atlantic City. I'd thrown that one away. Just because this one was bigger, was I going to make the same mistake?

Rising swiftly to my feet, I walked back down the aisle and through the front entrance, leaving the door open behind me. Standing on the cathedral steps, I looked around at the fall landscape. Trees rustled leaves hued orange, red, yellow, and even dark purple. A deep-blue sky overhead was dotted with flocks of fluffy, white clouds.

God, this is where you live! I directed heavenward. *I can see the life you've created. Leaves tossing in the breeze. Clouds floating across the sky. That isn't you inside there nailed to the church wall. You are out here in your creation.*

I looked back down the aisle at the crucifix on the far wall. Whatever its significance, it was not the living God I was looking for. Closing the door, I walked back to the bus station and went home. As I sat looking out the bus window, I came to a conclusion. I'd done everything I could think of to find a connection with God. Researching religions hadn't worked. Visiting churches hadn't worked. Statues and crucifixes had definitely not worked. So now it was over.

One last time, I retreated to my secret place and spoke to my invisible Friend. *God, when you saved me from the bombs, I was so sure you saved me for a purpose. I vowed I would find you and be your friend. But now I've done everything I can, and I still cannot find you. I don't know what else to do, so I'm just going to stop trying. If you have a purpose for my life, if you want to be my friend, then you will have to find me, because I don't know what to look for or where to look to find you.*

For the remainder of my high school years, I worked as hard at pushing away any more thoughts of God as I'd done with my loneliness, fear, and rejection during the war years. I told myself sternly, *Eleanor, you've got to stop looking for meaning in life. No one else at school talks like you do about searching for meaning. It's just making you old and unhappy, so that you don't fit in with the other girls your age.*

As with every aspect of my life, I formulated a plan. The best thing to do, I decided, was to make myself so busy I wouldn't have time to think about God or other weighty concepts like the meaning of life. It was now the beginning of my senior year of high school. I was still singing in the choir. By then I had a good reputation as a soloist. In fact, for my senior yearbook picture, I was named "The Voice". I was also carrying a full load of studies as well as cooking and cleaning at home and babysitting for pocket money.

But I still had too much time on my hands to keep from thinking. Going to the school principal, I asked, "Principal Halsey, is there any way I could be of help to you now that it is my senior year? I'm a good typist. Or maybe I could volunteer in the school office."

As might be expected, Principal Halsey was delighted at an offer of free help. "Just put a note up on the faculty bulletin board and say what you are willing to do."

I did so. The teachers were as delighted at my offer as Principal Halsey, and soon I was overwhelmed with requests to type up tests and other materials for history, English, math, French, agriculture, and music. I in turn was happy to be busy. Renting myself a typewriter, I set up an office down in the school basement under the stairs, where I would type up tests and other material. I also set up a home office in my bedroom with a table and lamp. What I couldn't finish at school, I'd take home and do at night. That still didn't keep me busy enough, so at lunch time I went to the cafeteria and asked how I could be of help.

"You can take over as cashier," the lunch lady told me.

So that became my job every lunch period. I also started preparing a lot of mimeographs. For twenty-first century readers who've never seen a mimeograph machine, this was in effect a primitive photocopier. It involved typing directly onto a special waxed paper, which punched out each letter, in effect turning the paper into a stencil. The stencil was run through the ink roll of the mimeograph machine, creating copies on regular paper.

Typing mimeographs brought me into the school office, since I had to come in early every morning to run off the mimeographs before class. Between coming in early, working into the evening, cooking dinner for the family, babysitting on weekends, homework, choir, and other school activities, I was finally too busy to think. Or to have any social life at all. The last thing I expected was that the biggest turning point of my life was just around the corner.

It started with the mimeographs. Since I had to deliver them to the school office every morning before class, I'd gotten to know two young women who worked there. Hilda was three years older than me, and Marian was two years older. They were also quite different than other young women I'd met. They dressed modestly and didn't wear bright lipstick or have pierced ears. They were always smiling and kind to me and had a gentle, sweet spirit about them.

Sometimes, when I came in early enough, I could see them gathered as though they were praying. I guessed that they were quite religious, though they never spoke of such to me. While I'd determined to stop searching, I found myself wondering what they believed. Then one day it all came to a head. I still remember the exact date—Thursday morning, February 25th, 1954.

I was working on the day's mimeographs when Marian entered the room. I can't remember what sparked the conversation, but I said to her, "Isn't it terrible what people do to God's beautiful world? All the bombing and war and abusing children, it's so sad!"

Marian just looked at me without saying a word. Then she picked up the printed mimeographs and walked out of the room. A little embarrassed, I thought to myself, *Well, I guess that's not a topic that interests her!* But the very next morning while I was running off mimeographs, Marian walked in with a Bible in her hand.

"I could tell you wanted to talk about God yesterday," she told me. "But I'm not allowed to bring up religion with students or anyone else during work hours. I came in early today, so we could talk before official office hours. Am I right that you're wanting to ask about God?"

"Oh, yes!" I answered fervently. "I've been searching for him since I was nine years old and the first bomb fell on my city."

She held up her Bible. "Well, did you know that Jesus Christ came into world just for you and that he loves you?"

I was stunned at her words. All these years of searching for an answer, and now here it was being laid simply and openly in front of me. Turning off the mimeograph machine,

I swung around to face Mariam, grabbed her by both shoulders, and said urgently, "I've been waiting to hear this for ten years. Please, tell me about it!".

Marian led me to a seat, opened up her Bible, and began to speak. She started in Genesis and told me about how God had created Adam and Eve. Then came the sad story of their disobedience and fall. A sinful humanity had been separated from their Creator ever since. That I had no problem understanding. I'd been witness to how much ugliness and evil human beings could perpetrate on each other. And I understood well that I too was a sinner and unworthy of God's mercy. But surely this despairing truth was not the message God had sent Marian to give me!

And it wasn't. Flipping the pages of her Bible to the New Testament, Marian read several verse from the book of Romans:

> For all have sinned and fall short of the glory of God, and all are justified freely by his grace through the redemption that came by Christ. Jesus
>
> —Romans 3:23-24

> For the wages of sin is death, but the gift of God is eternal life through Jesus Christ our Lord.
>
> —Romans 6:23

All have sinned. Yes, that included me. All are justified freely—by Christ Jesus? The gift of God is eternal life—

through Jesus Christ? This was the connection that had eluded me all these years between the God I'd been searching to know and the Jewish carpenter whom Christians revered.

But Marian wasn't finished. She turned the page and read another verse from the gospel of John. My heart began pounding as I listened:

> For God so loved the world that he gave his one and only Son, that whoever believes in him shall not perish but have eternal life. For God did not send his Son into the world to condemn the world, but to save the world through him.

> —John 3:16-17

"We've all sinned," Marian explained. "But since the first man and woman disobeyed their Creator, God has longed to restore his creation to himself. Out of his great love, he sent his only begotten Son Jesus Christ to die on the cross in our place, taking on himself the penalty for our sins. Because Jesus was sinless, he conquered death and rose from the dead. Do you believe this, Eleanor?"

I'd heard bits and pieces of this story in church services and Christmas programs. But never in such a way that made sense. I immediately realized that I did believe it—all of it. Not just because it sounded so logical, but because something in me recognized it as truth. I know now the Holy Spirit was speaking to my heart.

Grabbing Marian's hand in mine, I answered, "Do I believe it? This is exactly what I've been seeking for so many years.

I've looked high and low all over the world, searching for how I could connect with God. But I could never find him."

Marian smiled warmly at me. "You don't need to find him, Eleanor. He has found you."

Tears filled my eyes. This was exactly what I'd begged God to do when I'd given up on my search. In fact, so many of the things I'd thought and questions I'd wondered about were being answered in the words Marian was reading.

Marian seemed to sense what I was feeling. Gently, she said, "Eleanor, God doesn't just love the whole world. He loves you. If you were the only person on this earth, he'd still have sent his Son to die for you. That's how much he loves you."

Those were magical words to me. Everything I'd ever stored away in my child's heart about my invisible Friend, all the questions and longing I'd felt for so many years past, it was all coming together and making sense. It almost seemed too easy and too good to be true.

"Let's read John 3:16 again," Marian went on. "But this time let's make it personal. You see, we can talk about God. We can go to church. We can learn about Jesus. We can even celebrate his birth at Christmas. But we can't make a connection with him until we make it personal."

That made sense to me. It was rather like getting married. You could have a boyfriend and even know all about him. But you would not be actually bound together in holy matrimony until you were willing to say in front of the minister, "I, Eleanor, take you, So-and-So, to be my husband."

"Okay, I'm going to hand you my Bible. I want you to read the verse for yourself, and this time say your own name every place it talks about the world."

I took the Bible and read the words as she directed: "For God so loved **Eleanor** that he gave his one and only Son, that if **Eleanor** believes in him, **Eleanor** shall not perish but have eternal life. For God did not send his Son into the world to condemn **Eleanor**, but to save **Eleanor** through him (John 3:16-17)."

The words sang in my heart. It was all now so clear, so personal. This was the purpose for which God had saved me from the bombs. This was what I'd spent so long seeking. And so it was that at 8:45 a.m., on February 25th, 1954, I gave my life to Christ. I was now connected to my Creator, beloved daughter of the King of Kings, a follower of Jesus Christ.

My physical birthday had never meant much to me, representative as it was of parents who'd never wanted me. But my spiritual birthday into the family of God is a day I still celebrate joyously every year. Sixty-three years later, the rapturous wonder of that moment has not worn off, and I am sure it never will!

CHAPTER SEVENTEEN

FOUND

For God did not send his Son into the world to condemn the world, but to save the world through him.

—John 3:17

Once I'd finished praying, Marian had to resume her duties and I had to finish the mimeographs. I was still thinking, *If this is it, it's awfully easy!* As Marian left the room, I called after her, "Are you sure there isn't something more I need to do?"

Turning, she smiled at me. "No, Eleanor. Jesus did it all for you. All you have to do is believe it."

My first morning class was English. I walked there, still wondering, *Okay, God, do I give you money? Go to church? What do I do next?* The following day, Marian approached me to ask, "Would you like to go to church with me on Sunday?"

I did attend church with Marian. I don't remember what the pastor preached about, but something in his message settled my thoughts because I walked out of the service absolutely convinced I'd found what I'd been searching for all my life. As Marian had assured me, there was nothing more I need do but believe what Jesus Christ had done for me.

Monday, I went to school bubbling over with excitement. Every acquaintance I ran into, I accosted with the words, "Guess what! I've found him!"

"Who have you found?" they kept asking me. "Do you have a boyfriend? Are you getting married?"

"No, I've found a connection with the God of the universe," I answered.

Eventually, I ran into my music teacher. When I told her how I'd finally found meaning in life, she frowned. "You've clearly been talking to those girls in the office. They aren't supposed to be proselytizing students. I'm going to have to report this to the principal."

"No, no!" I assured her. "This wasn't their doing. I've been looking for a relationship with God since the first bomb fell on our town in Germany. Now God has found me, and I've come to know Jesus in a personal way. Please don't report them."

She reluctantly let the matter go. The only people I didn't tell about my changed life were my mother and stepfather. I didn't think they'd understand. But they soon saw a change in me since my new faith transformed my attitude and behavior. I continued attending church with Marian. Though not a large church, it had a very active group of young adults. One of them was Hilda, who worked in the school office with Marian. Another was a girl from my own class, Dolores, who was being mentored spiritually by Hilda. Marian became my own mentor and spiritual mother.

The four of us were always together and became close friends, though we were very different in personality and background. Hilda was a joyful, outgoing girl, always well-groomed and well-dressed. In contrast, Marian was always serious and uninterested in frivolities like fashion, make-up or hairstyles. My classmate Dolores was also outgoing and very pretty from a well-off, upper-class family. She even had her own convertible. She'd occasionally invite me for a ride with the roof down, a real treat.

But it was difficult for me to relate to Dolores or vice versa. She'd grown up in a loving home with every want granted. My background was so different and dark. Still, I was grateful to finally have friends who let me be part of their group. I'd never been able to bond with other people. But I was now learning what it meant to be a loved member of a real family, the family of God.

My life now revolved around church as well as school. I attended youth group, Bible study, Wednesday night prayer meeting, as well as Sunday services. My mother and stepfather never questioned my activities. So long as I didn't get into trouble, they didn't care where I was or what I was doing. The Bible became my favorite book. I read it, studied it, and memorized countless Bible verses. I especially loved those that spoke of God as our father:

> ➤ A father to the fatherless . . . is God in his holy dwelling (Psalm 68:5).

> ➤ As a father has compassion on his children, so the Lord has compassion on those who fear him (Psalm 103:13).

> ➤ You, Lord, are our Father, our Redeemer from of old is your name (Isaiah 63:16).

Every time I found such a verse, I would write it out. There were so many of them, I lost count. Reading and rereading them alone in my room, I'd cry aloud, "Oh, God, it really is all true! I don't have to make believe you are my daddy because you were all the time. Or that my invisible Friend really did love me because you've loved me before I ever knew you."

Learning about my heavenly Father was like stepping out of that dark, dank cave where we'd cowered from bombs into the sunlight of a bright, fresh spring morning. To this point, my life had felt a jumble of mismatched, purposeless puzzle pieces. Once I gave my life to Jesus, the pieces suddenly fit together to become a beautiful mosaic. Even the dark, lonely parts of my life, all that I'd endured in the war, the rejection and pain, had all played a part in leading me to my heavenly Father.

This is a truth I pray that you, my dear reader, will take to heart. God has a pattern he is creating for each of our lives out of both the good and bad, the bright colors and the dark hues. If we can just recognize this truth and trust God with our lives, what joy and peace we will experience!

That June, I graduated from high school with high honors and as a member of the National Honor Society. I found myself somewhat embarrassed when my teachers held me up as an example to American-born students, saying, "This girl Eleanor only came to the States and learned English just five years ago, and she gets straight As. What's wrong with you kids?"

I'd received a scholarship offer for four years of college. But when I told my mother, she was strongly opposed. Like her sister Lisbeth, Mom saw little value in education, especially for a woman.

"You don't need college!" she told me bluntly. "Just get a job so you can start earning money and support yourself."

I am sorry now that I listened to her. But I did. I found a job as a secretarial assistant at an insurance company. I took two buses each way to reach my job, so I used my time on the bus to study the Bible. I also read Christian classics—A. W. Tozer, Charles Spurgeon, Harry A. Ironside, Andrew Murray. Just as I'd done with my English "dictionary", I started writing down in notebooks everything I was learning.

Then a new challenge entered my life. Just a few months after I came to Christ, I was attending a wedding with the rest of our "foursome" when someone said to me, "Eleanor, I think you're losing your hearing. We weren't talking just now about stairs. We were talking about pears in the salad. I think you need to have your hearing checked out!"

Oh, no, what now? rushed into my mind. I'd never been on a date, and while I was no longer particularly plump, my self-image of someone too fat and ugly to ever have a boyfriend was still firmly in my mind. So I never really considered a future that held a husband or children. Still, I remember clearly my first real prayer after accepting Jesus as my Savior:

Okay, God, now that you have found me and I am connected to you, please don't bring me a husband until all my emotional problems are solved. I am still such a mess, and I don't want to bring any of my traumatic slush into marriage. Also, I want to get to know you well before anything else. So whatever you need to do in my life to bring me close to you, it's okay.

Well, dear reader, don't ask God to do something in your life unless you mean business! The very next day, I made an appointment with a hearing specialist. He discovered I had advanced otosclerosis, which is a buildup of calcium around the stapes, a tiny bone inside the ear, which prevents the normal transmission of sound. Many factors can cause otosclerosis. But one major cause is prolonged exposure to extreme noise such as constantly listening to earsplitting music or working around noisy machinery.

My own situation could have derived from years of bomb blasts or some hereditary factor. But the specialist was not optimistic. "You'll be stone-deaf in two years. Maybe less."

My reaction was not what he expected. In fact, I rather surprised myself when I turned with a smile to Marian, who'd accompanied me. "Well, it looks like God has answered my very first prayer. Now I won't be able to hear anyone but him!"

I meant it with all my heart. But that didn't make the next few years easy. As prognosticated, I lost all hearing in well under two years. As with every challenge in my life, I chose to seek out the positive. If God had permitted this, then he could bring something good out of it. Starting with my job. I could hardly perform my responsibilities as a secretarial assistant without being able to hear, so I went to my employer and explained the situation. Like so many encouraging people God has brought into my life, she was a wonderful, kindly woman.

"Don't worry," she told me. "We'll let you handle the Dictaphone machine, with the volume turned all the way up."

A Dictaphone was a small cassette recorder used to take down letters and other spoken material for transcription. Typing up all those transcripts became my full-time job. A hearing aid made this possible. Nothing like today's tiny devices, this was a metallic box, three inches by five inches, from which a wire rose to Walkman-style earphones. The device allowed me to handle transcriptions and follow conversations, but it was clunky and ugly and made me very self-conscious.

Also, because I couldn't hear clearly, I developed a stutter. It became easier not to talk at all, so I retreated even deeper into my inner self. When I was alone, it didn't matter that I couldn't hear. I could still watch a beautiful sunset, smell a flower, enjoy the innocent smile of a baby in a passing stroller. I could also read, so I buried myself in Christian books and reading my Bible. Much like the secret place to which I'd retreated as a child, the silence in which I lived became my own spiritual sanctuary where I communed with God.

CHAPTER EIGHTEEN

SANCTUARY

Be still before the Lord and wait patiently for him.

—Psalm 37:7a

I needed the inner peace of that sanctuary because my outer life wasn't always easy or happy. My mother and stepfather weren't really talking to me, though I still lived at home. They felt I was too religious and not just because I was constantly at church. Marian had been my spiritual mentor since I'd come to Christ. I loved her dearly and accepted without question everything she taught me. This included very strict policies against anything she considered "worldly" such as wearing makeup, earrings, or pants. For a woman to cut her hair, wear bright colors, or do anything that attracted attention was being a "Jezebel", one of the Bible's most infamous pagan queens (I Kings 16).

It never occurred to me to question Marian's interpretation of Scripture, so I followed her tenets as closely as I could. I can still visualize the Eleanor of my mid-twenties. Messy, untrimmed curls. No makeup. Unfashionable clothing worn loose to hide the clunky hearing mechanism strapped to my chest.

I not only felt ugly, but old beyond my years. I was also very shy, afraid to talk due to my stutter, and so self-conscious that if I so much as mumbled a greeting, my neck would break out in red blotches. Our "foursome" was my one lifeline. Others in the youth group were getting married and having babies. But Marian, Hilda, and Dolores weren't dating either, and I still spent my free time with them. I tried hard to fit in, copying their mannerisms, laughing when they laughed, however old and solemn I felt. I even accompanied Marian on mission trips to Canada, where we taught Vacation Bible School in the small towns and countryside of rural Alberta.

Those ten years of deafness are what today I call my quiet years. One day I was reading a passage written by the Old Testament prophet Joel. The passage was written to the nation of Israel at a time when they'd gone through great sorrow and loss. Phrases jumped out at me as I read:

> Be glad, people of Zion, rejoice in the Lord your God . . . I [God] will repay you for the years the locusts have eaten . . . and you will praise the name of the Lord your God, who has worked wonders for you . . . you will know that I am in Israel, that I am the Lord your God, and that there is no other.
>
> —Joel 2:23-27

As I read the words, I remember vividly praying: *God, I will never get married or have children. Who'd want me with my messy hair, hearing aid, and stutter? But even the darkest moments are better than when I was in Germany because now I know you. Maybe these quiet years are necessary so my roots will sink deep down into your love. But even from this, you can create something good and beautiful. And you've promised to repay all the years the locusts have eaten. That means somewhere in future you will restore to me the childhood and youth I've never had. I can't even guess how. But in the meantime, I give to you my stuttering tongue and my life as it is. And I am going to trust you to make them into something good and beautiful.*

I will tell you later, dear reader, how God answered that prayer. But now comes a difficult part of my story. I dearly loved my "foursome". They were the first real family I'd had in my life. Still, the more I studied the Bible, prayed, and shared my faith with others, especially those who knew nothing about God and church, as I'd been when Marian led me to Christ, the more disillusioned I became with Marian's view of serving God. The Jesus I saw in Scripture was not a churchy person. He was always willing to spend time with sinners and non-believers. He taught far less about how to dress or act religiously than about caring for the lost and touching others with God's love.

When Marian first led me to Christ, I was grateful to learn the basics of Christianity from her. But I was no longer a brand-new believer, while Marian still expected me to follow anything she told me. Much though I loved her, I was beginning to rebel against her assumption of authority over my life. If I dared disagree with her or veered from her rules, she vociferously expressed her disapproval.

This all came to a head one day when I bought a new coat. A burgundy-red coat. I needed the coat and had saved my own earnings for it. So it never occurred to me that its purchase involved any spiritual issue. Sunday morning, I happily wore the coat to church, feeling quite positive for a change about my appearance.

But the moment I walked into the church lobby, Marian began berating me. "Eleanor, do you know how worldly you look in that coat? You know what the Bible says about man looking on the outside, but God looking on the heart (1 Samuel 16:7)."

I was crushed. But I was also feeling rebellious. I asked her bluntly, "So if I wear this same coat in black, it's spiritual? But in red it's worldly?"

She responded with a lecture on the sin of attracting attention to myself. I didn't argue, but from that day our friendship took a different turn. Marian was a good, devout Christian woman, and I loved her dearly. But I could no longer obey her blindly.

Yes, God looks on the heart and man looks on the outside! I thought to myself. *But if men do look on the outside, then how is going around with my outside looking dowdy and unattractive going to make them want to listen to me tell them about God?*

I kept wearing the burgundy-red coat, not in defiance or anger against Marian, but because I'd come to see clearly that many of her decrees were no more from Scripture than those of the Pharisees Jesus had decried (Matthew 23). Legalism is the term given to man-made laws purported to prove one's spirituality. I'd grown in my faith enough to recognize that God was calling his children to show love, compassion, kindness, and other fruits of the Spirit (Galatians 5:22-23), not just dress a certain way or avoid jewelry and makeup.

I had no idea then that my quiet years were about to end. Then one day, my boss said to me, "Eleanor, did you know there are two new operations called a 'fenestration' and 'stapedectomy' that can restore hearing in some deaf people? Why don't you make an appointment and see if your condition would qualify for the operation?"

I'd never heard of such procedures, but I took her suggestion as a direct message from God. My boss actually set up the appointment and gave me the day off to travel into New York City to the doctor's office. There I learned that my condition of otosclerosis made me a perfect candidate for both surgeries. Fenestration is simply drilling a hole into the skull and sewing skin from your hand over the opening, thus creating a window into the brain that is similar to the eardrum. A stapedectomy is a procedure that replaces the small bones in the ear that transmit sound (hammer, anvil, and stapes) then substituting plastic parts. These procedures take one hour while you are awake, after which you go home. My health insurance would even cover much of the cost.

So at the age of twenty-nine after ten years of silence, I went into the hospital for the operation. This proved a complete success with 85-90% of my hearing restored.

While I was there, my mother came to visit me. In all my quiet years, Mom had never acknowledged my deafness. Perhaps this was once again guilt, as if I'd lost my hearing due to all the bombs, then she was at least partially responsible. So she insisted I wasn't actually deaf. I just didn't listen.

Which meant my operation wasn't really necessary either. When Mom arrived at the hospital, I had thick bandages covering the surgical site. It was raining outside, and Mom complained about how hard it had been for her to take a bus in a thunderstorm to come see me. Only then did she bother glancing at my bandages

"I still think you just don't listen!" she informed me with a sniff.

I refused to allow her disapproval to put a damper on my joy. How does one express in mere words what it felt like to be able to hear after ten years of silence? I hadn't realized how little I'd been catching even with my hearing aid. Now I couldn't get enough of sound. Music on the radio. The melodies of bird song and rushing of water. The shrill bark of a dog. The noise of buses and cars in the street. I even jumped at the sound of placing my teacup into the saucer.

My last follow-up visit to the doctor's office was on a workday afternoon. My boss again gave me the time off. As I sat in the waiting room, I prayed, *Okay, God, now I have my hearing back. So what am I going to do with this shy, stuttering Eleanor inside me? I want to be a beautiful woman whose life brings glory to you. I want to share your love and your words with others now that I can hear again. But how can I learn to be a beautiful woman?*

I'd been leafing through a magazine while I waited. Just as I finished praying, I glanced down. Words on the page jumped out at me: "Are you shy? Are you nervous around the public? Are you afraid of speaking to people? Then give us a call."

It was an ad for the John Roberts Power School of Charm, which included a modeling agency, a finishing school, and classes for actors. I asked the doctor's receptionist if I could use the office phone, then called the number in the ad. As I did so, I prayed, *I have no social graces, God. If you showed me this ad for a reason, then please give me a sign this is from you. If this will help me, then let it be affordable. Let there be transportation from Kenilworth so I can attend!*

To my excitement, the school had a ten-week course starting that Saturday for just $200. The location was in New Jersey on a direct bus route from New York City to Montclair. I signed up immediately. Coming to know Jesus had completely transformed my inner self. That charm course transformed my outer self. We learned hair and skin care, wardrobe planning and color coordination, good posture, how to shake hands properly, maintain eye contact, and speak assertively. We also learned that self-confidence is something you learn, not that you are born with.

"No matter how shy you are," the instructor taught us, "if you know how to stand properly in public with good posture and eye contact, no one will know you are nervous."

I drank in every word. By the fifth session, I had learned enough about proper wardrobe coordination that I went out and bought a spring-pink dress suit with matching patent leather shoes, panty hose, long, white gloves, and a black hat with a long feather. I had my dark curls trimmed into the latest style.

That Sunday, I applied makeup as I'd been taught—not made-up, but made-down—for a natural look. In my pink suit, I walked into the church lobby. There I struck a pose exactly as I'd learned in class, posture straight, heel of one foot tucked into the arch of the other. Jaws literally dropped open all over the lobby. People kept coming up to ask, "Eleanor, is that really you? What happened?"

I count that day my "coming out" as a debutante. Or rather, as a beautiful daughter of the King of kings. Never again did I see people snickering at my frizzy hair, stuttering, or anything else I did. From that moment on, I blossomed into the fresh, youthful womanhood that all the years of war and deafness had stolen from me. God had indeed repaid the years the locusts had eaten!

Chapter Nineteen

Daughter of the King

I can do all things through Christ who strengthens me.

—Philippians 4:13

After that church lobby performance, people started treating me differently and they began calling me "Elegant Ellie." At twenty-nine-years old, I was on my way to catch up on everything I'd missed. While it took me some time to get used to this new, confident Eleanor, anything now seemed possible. I had come to recognize I was not just loved by God, but that as his daughter, he had created me to be an example of beautiful womanhood. Instead of hiding from people and cowering from life, I could do all things through Christ.

By the time I finished the charm course, I'd learned to deliver a public speech, had a new wardrobe, and felt more comfortable around others. People began including me in their social activities. This included Dolores, who'd been part of our foursome, but always ran in a more affluent, socially-active crowd than the rest of us. She taught me to ski and would invite me to accompany her on ski trips to resorts in Canada and New England.

Through Dolores and her friends, I met a Christian man who was a New York City planner. He was planning a trip to Europe and offered to take a group of us along as his students. The trip lasted for three weeks, and we visited thirteen countries. While we had to pay our own travel expenses, it was a wonderful opportunity. Luxemburg put on a night light show just for us. We went skiing at the top of the Swiss Alps. In Rotterdam, Germany, their city planner entertained us for lunch on a private yacht.

This was my first trip back to Germany, and I was stunned to see everything rebuilt and prosperous with no signs left of the war. Eastern Germany was still sealed off behind the Soviet Iron Curtain, so I wasn't able to visit my old home. But just hearing German for the first time in years pulled me sharply back into childhood memories.

With my hearing restored, my employment life opened up as well. No longer confined to transcribing Dictaphone tapes, I was soon promoted to personal secretary, or administrative assistant, as it is termed today. Over the next years, I accepted promotions to serve as personal secretary to several prominent businessmen. I also began taking night classes, working towards my bachelor's degree, though with a full-time job I could only take a few credits each year.

In all this, I hadn't abandoned what I'd learned spiritually during the quiet years. I was still studying my Bible and active in church. I taught a fourth-grade Sunday school class. I'd also started singing again, as I hadn't been able to do while deaf. I took voice lessons and was soon being hired to sing at weddings, banquets, and churches. My desire in all this was to do what I'd prayed for during my quiet years—that God would use me as an instrument to help others, especially those who had gone through similar trials of rejection and hardship.

Two years into my new life, I decided it was time to move into my own apartment. At the age of thirty-one, I'd never lived alone before, and it was a great delight to create my own home. I organized my closets and cupboards as I'd been taught in charm school. I started a library with lots of books on history, charm, self-confidence as well as Christian classics.

Since I now had space to entertain, I often invited friends over for dinner. I learned to set a proper table. I purchased cookbooks and tried out new recipes. I also joined a gym to keep my body healthy and fit. By now I had my own vehicle, a Volkswagen bug, so I felt completely independent and free. In all, life was beautiful. The darkness of my early years had faded, and I was enjoying to the hilt all God had restored to me.

By this time, I was working for a company called Celanese Corporation. Celanese later merged with the German company Hoechst to form the largest chemical company in the world. But even then, it was a very large company specializing in chemical, pharmaceutical, plastic polymer, and engineering products. A year after starting work there, I was promoted to be the personal assistant of one of the directors, Dr. P. R. Lantos.

The promotion wasn't just because of my administrative skills. I'd maintained the lessons I learned at charm school, always dressing impeccably and projecting a confident demeanor. In fact, when photographers came in to produce commercials for new products, I was asked to model for several advertisements. I could now mingle with company executives and their guests with complete self-assurance.

Around this same time, Celanese began accepting applications for new managers. As Dr. Lantos' personal secretary, I handled the paperwork. One résumé in particular greatly impressed me. Dr. Robert Isaacson had earned his PhD in biochemistry by age twenty-three and had eighteen registered pharmaceutical patents by age twenty-eight. He was now in his early thirties. In fact, exactly my age. He came in for an interview and was immediately hired.

Now, dear reader, you have probably already guessed from his name that Bob Isaacson eventually became my husband. It was not love at first sight for either of us. For my part, I greatly admired Bob. Part of my duties for Dr. Lantos was scheduling staff meetings, which meant I had to call each manager. Bob had a wonderful sense of humor and would always make me laugh. I enjoyed our conversations, and he certainly seemed to enjoy talking with me, since our phone calls soon became much longer than necessary. When the management staff went out for lunch, Bob and I found plenty to talk about. He liked that I was always seeking to learn new things and pursue personal growth.

But one issue kept us apart. God had brought me through a long, dark tunnel to find faith, light, and redemption in Jesus Christ. Though of Jewish heritage, Bob Isaacson was not religious at all. Still, he didn't mind when I shared my own faith with him. He'd ask how I'd spent my weekend, and I'd answer back, "Well, I'm teaching a Sunday school class on the life of Moses. I love reading the Torah, as you call the first five Old Testament books. What do you think of them?"

Bob had been hired at Celanese in 1967. By 1970, I'd been working there four years and was finding myself bored with my position as a personal secretary. It wasn't that I disliked my work or my colleagues, but in every job I'd held, I'd learned as much as I could, then moved on to something more challenging. I now felt I had learned all I could by working for Dr. Lantos. Dr. Lantos also told me he was planning to leave the company, so I began looking around for new employment opportunities.

By now, I was practiced at job interviews. I received a call from a gas company owned by Mr. Kean, scion of a well-known New Jersey political family, whose members included congressmen, senators, governors, and other prominent politicians all the way back to George Washington and the Declaration of Independence. Their personnel director had been very impressed with my résumé and wanted to set up an interview.

I'd done some research into the Kean family, so I knew just how prominent they were. New Jersey even has a university and museum named after famous Kean family members. But I determined I was not going to sound over-eager when I called back.

"I'm sorry, but I can't take off from work for an interview," I told the woman who answered the phone. "If your personnel director wants to meet with me, he'll have to schedule it in the evening after I get off work."

"I'll check and get back to you," she responded. The next day she called back. "My employer is willing to make an exception for your interview. Here is the time and place."

My confidence was high as I walked into the conference room, immaculately groomed and wearing a beautiful forest-green three-piece knit suit. That's when I discovered I wasn't just meeting the personnel director, but the company president, Mr. Kean, and his vice-president as well. Mr. Kean's office was imposing with its beautiful cherry wood furniture, white couches, and real fireplace that could be turned on with a remote. Now it felt more like facing a firing squad. But I took my seat with composure and began answering questions.

They seemed happy with my response. I in turn refused to be overawed by their descriptions of how prestigious my job would be, the top salary I'd earn, and the beautiful office I'd have with a solid teak desk and plants. After the interview, they asked me to wait outside the conference room while they discussed the matter. They called me back a few minutes later.

"We've decided to offer you the position," Mr. Kean informed me.

I could see they were expecting me to be overwhelmed at their generosity. Instead, I looked at them coolly. "Thank you very much for the offer. I'll have to think about it and let you know."

Where did I get the courage for such a response? Only the new Eleanor could have conjured it up! They all looked surprised. Then Mr. Kean said, "Well, let us know as soon as you can."

In truth, I was already confident I would take the job. But I'd learned to take everything to God first, and I wanted time to pray about it. Driving home, I lifted my thoughts in prayer.

God, we need to talk! In all my other jobs, I've been very free about sharing my faith. But now I'm taking on a very prestigious position working for the company president himself. I can't just go sharing my faith with everyone who walks into his office like I do now. He wouldn't appreciate that. So would it be okay with you in this new job if I'm no longer a Christian secretary, but a secretary who just happens to also be a Christian?

Dearest reader, I can tell you now this was the biggest mistake I ever made since I'd become a Christian. You see, God is a gentleman. When we choose to kick God out of our lives in any way, he will move out. He won't stay where he isn't wanted. But believe me, when we do that, Fate always comes marching in, and sooner or later, we'll find ourselves paying for the consequences.

It wasn't long before I discovered that for myself!

CHAPTER TWENTY

RESTORATION

Whoever acknowledges me [Jesus] before others, I
will also acknowledge before my Father in heaven.
But whoever disowns me before others, I will disown
before my Father in heaven.

—Matthew 10:32-33

The next morning, I gave my two-weeks' notice at
Celanese, and for the next six years, I worked as Mr.
Kean's personal secretary. But I never had the feeling
of fulfillment I'd enjoyed in my prior job. I blamed this on my
new environment. At Celanese, I'd been surrounded by
highly intelligent, interesting people. Most employees I dealt
with had PhDs.

In my new position, none of my colleagues had been to
college or even cared about such things. My boss presented
a handsome, well-appointed image. But he'd inherited his
position because of his family name, not due to personal
ability or hard work.

One bright spot in my life was Bob Isaacson. By now he'd
been promoted to Director of Advanced Science and

Technology at Celanese. I'd missed our conversations, and he clearly had too, because he called to ask me for a date. I still remember that night vividly. Bob took me to the iconic Rainbow Room restaurant on the 65th floor of the Rockefeller Center in Manhattan, then to a Spanish restaurant, followed by a performance of the Bolshoi Ballet at Lincoln Center, finishing off the evening with desert at the famous Russian Tearoom.

We had a wonderful evening. Bob treated me like a princess, his conversation intelligent and humorous. He in turn expressed interest in my college classes, singing engagements, and other activities. I knew I looked elegant in a sophisticated white knit dress with black trim, patent-leather pumps, and purse.

"Thank you for the evening," Bob told me when he dropped me off at my apartment. "I really enjoyed it. I hope we can do this again."

"That would be great," I responded.

And that was the end of it. Bob and I remained good friends, and I continued to accept occasional date invitations. I also had other male acquaintances who took me out to dinner and other social functions, but only as casual friends.

I'd instituted one other change. As I matured in my faith, I'd become convicted at what the Bible teaches about honoring our father and mother (Deuteronomy 5:16; Ephesians 6:2). I'd achieved a reasonably peaceable relationship with my mother. But I hadn't seen my father since I was thirteen. One day, I tracked Pop down at his work and asked if I could visit him. He sounded surprised, but gave me his current address, a forty-five-minute drive from my apartment.

Pop also informed me with great pride that I now had a half-brother named Johnny. That brought a pang of hurt, as I'd never forgotten Mom telling me how disappointed Pop was that I'd been born a girl. As I drove to his house, I reminded myself sternly, *You're doing this out of obedience to God, not just to feel good!*

When I arrived at Pop's house, I was so nervous I had to muster enough courage to force myself out of the car. But Pop proved quite cordial, though his first words were, "You sure look like your mother!"

Since they didn't get along at all, I don't think he meant it for a compliment. Pop took me inside to meet his son Johnny, a nice-enough young man in his teens. I visited courteously with Pop's wife Billie. From then on, I drove up there once a month. I would bring them gifts and chat amicably. They never visited me in turn, and we never developed any real relationship. But at least my conscience was clear that I'd made peace with my father as much as was possible for me to do.

Meanwhile, I was becoming more and more unhappy with my job. I was earning good money and living a comfortable lifestyle. In fact, I was living the very life of art, culture, and elegance to which I'd aspired since Frau Benner and my friend Maria's family had introduced me to such possibilities. But I was also beginning to feel as empty and without purpose as when I'd been a little girl in Germany.

My boss always took a month off in August to go safari hunting in Africa, which left me with little to do. I took a Dale Carnegie public speaking course, then a ten-week course at the Barbizon School of Modeling and Personal Improvement. I began modeling for Barbizon in my free time. I was also receiving invitations to speak about my childhood experiences in WWII. I'd started teaching a Bible study.

I continued working on my bachelor's degree. During a psychology course, I was given a personality analysis. After grading it, the professor told me, "Eleanor, secretarial work is not the right career for you. With your outgoing personality, you should be in sales." *Ha ha*, I thought. He never knew how shy I really was inside.

I was so surprised. Despite my new, self-confident public persona, I'd always thought of myself as a shy, introverted person by nature. The psychology course helped me realize it was actually the other way around. All the years of rejection, loneliness, and war, followed by years of deaf solitude, had turned inward what was in fact the bubbly, sociable personality with which God had actually created me. That realization helped me turn my back permanently on the shy, reclusive Eleanor to become the outgoing, people-oriented extrovert God had designed me to be.

But this realization made me even less happy with my job. It wasn't so much that I disliked the work as that I was just plain bored. I'd come to love the modeling, singing, and public speaking that brought me into contact with other people. Being cooped up at an office desk was no longer satisfying. I began looking around for new career opportunities, but nothing I found made me feel any less empty.

It was then that I came to realize just why I was so unhappy. This wasn't just because of my secretarial duties. It was because I'd deliberately chosen to push God out of this job. As I said earlier, God is a gentleman, and when we choose to push him away, he will leave. Since the day Marian had introduced me to the heavenly Father I'd sought so many years, I'd never pushed him out of any aspect of my life. But now I was living as though he was no longer my Lord and King. Yes, I was still attending church, even teaching a Bible study. But in my job and personal life, I'd stop giving God first place. How could I expect God to acknowledge me when I had stopped acknowledging him before others?

This was March, 1973. Sitting at my desk, I prayed repentantly, *God, I am so sorry I kicked you out of this job. I need you, and I want to come back to you. Please forgive me! And if you want me to stay in this job, please give me a love for my job and the respect I need for my boss. But I'm done trying to rearrange my life on my own.*

My thoughts went to that long-ago day when I had given up on my search for God and had prayed that God would instead find me. Fervently, I added, *God, I'm not going to go looking for any more job interviews. If you have a job for me, then I am going to trust you bring it to me.*

Dear reader, you may think that what happened next is too improbable to have happened, or maybe that I've made it up to embellish the story. But I promise it is the unvarnished truth. Just as I finished praying, the phone rang. On the line was the owner of the Barbizon School of Modeling.

"Eleanor, I've been thinking about you," he said. "I need a new director of admissions at the school. With your skills, you'd be perfect for the job. I'll be here till 9 p.m. Why don't you come on up, and we'll talk."

I knew without doubt this was God's merciful answer to my prayer. By that evening, I'd accepted the job offer and given my notice at the gas company. Over the following months, I had never been happier. Not just because I loved my new job, but because I was again putting God first in my life.

Along with handling admissions, I continued doing some modeling for Barbizon. I also began teaching some of their courses. During this time, I was still seeing Bob Isaacson. In his job, Bob traveled all over the world, but when he was in town on a Saturday, he would invite me out. He was always looking for new ideas to make our dates special. One year he took me to all the restaurants on top of famous New York City skyscrapers like the Rockefeller Center and the Empire State Building. The next year we did the rounds of lower-down restaurants like Cave and King Louis XVI.

Bob admired my decision to branch into a new career and encouraged me in every way. We'd become very close friends, though we were opposites in many ways. He was the true scientist, thoughtful, intellectual, and reserved. I was the outgoing, bubbly one. But when he was with me, I helped him become more outgoing and he helped me to settle down.

Still, one thing continued to separate us. I knew I could never go beyond friendship with someone who didn't share my faith. For his part, Bob had never met a Christian like me who spoke openly of my faith. Many times, I would share with him my assurance that Jesus was the Messiah prophesied by the Old Testament Jewish prophets. He didn't object to this, since he was very much a person who didn't interfere with how others lived or what they believed. He simply didn't accept such faith for himself.

One day, Bob told me bluntly, "I don't think I could ever have the faith you have. But I admire the way you have so much strength, peace, and purpose because of your faith."

Still, Bob was very open intellectually and a big reader. By now we were good enough friends that we always exchanged Christmas gifts. So in 1973, I gave him a beautiful, leather-bound Bible for Christmas. As he opened my gift, I clarified quickly, "I'm not trying to push my faith on you. I just want you to have this for your library, since you keep expressing how much you admire my life, and anything I am and do is because of this book."

Bob expressed polite appreciation, but said little more about my gift. Over the following year, we continued to see each other when he was in New York. That next Christmas of 1974, we once again exchanged gifts. I'd given him a tie. He gave me a bracelet. But after we opened our gifts, he handed me another box, beautifully wrapped. When I opened it, I found inside the Bible I'd given him the Christmas before.

"Oh, what is this?" I asked in dismay. "Did you not want this in your library?"

"Just open it," he responded with a smile.

I opened the Bible. On the front leaf, he had written neatly, "I, Robert Isaacson, have accepted Jesus Christ as my Savior and Messiah, and I will live for him the rest of my days with Eleanor's help."

Stunned, I re-read the words. Then I looked up at him. "Why are you doing this? Are you sure?"

I will admit I was concerned at first that he might have written these words to please me. But he said strongly, "Yes, I'm sure. Eleanor, I've always admired the strength and peace and purpose you have that is outside your own self. I've known for some time that it was right for me to do this."

"But when did this happen?" I asked, bewildered.

Bob then explained that for some time he'd been reading the Bible I gave him. As he'd read, he'd come to accept that I was right and that Jesus was indeed his Messiah. He went on, "Back in August, I was flying home from a business trip from California. While I was up in the air, it hit me that I had no purpose for living the way you do. Whether I lived or died, my life had no meaning. That was when I prayed and asked Jesus to be my Savior and Messiah. I wanted to surprise you for Christmas. Now do you think you could teach me all you know about the Bible and Jesus?"

Well, he'd certainly surprised me! I was overjoyed that my dear friend had found the Savior who'd transformed my own life. It wasn't till later when I remembered that long-ago encounter on the streets of Plauen when my childish heart had determined that one day when I grew up, I would marry a man from the people group who wore that pretty gold six-pointed star on their sleeve.

CHAPTER TWENTY-ONE

JOYOUS UNION

Forgetting what is behind and straining toward what is ahead, I press on toward the goal to win the prize for which God has called me heavenward in Christ Jesus.

—Philippians 3:13b-14

Though not much later, since by the end of January, Bob asked me to marry him, and I accepted. As he'd requested, I'd begun teaching him about the Bible. I took him to visit my own church as well as others in the area. We hadn't yet set a wedding date when Bob asked me, "So where would you like to live, Sweets?"

"Sweets" had become his term of endearment for me, and he rarely again ever called me Eleanor. There was a very exclusive community called Short Hills not far away in New Jersey where I'd always wished I could live. We toured the area and found a beautiful eleven-room home. Bob put a deposit down, but I was beginning to feel nervous. We were both forty years old, and neither of us had been married.

We'd had such a wonderful relationship as friends. Would that change if we married?

God, am I doing the right thing here? I prayed in a panic. I told Bob, "I think I need to pray about this some more."

Bob called the realtor and put a hold on the house purchase. We didn't talk further for two weeks. Then one evening I accepted his invitation to dinner. At the restaurant, he looked at me sadly. "Sweets, I think I've lost you!"

I could see from his troubled expression that he thought I'd accepted his invitation so I could break up with him. Quickly, I reassured him, "No, Bob, I want to get married to you. There is no one else I'd ever want to marry."

I realized just how true it was. Many years earlier in my romantic youth, I'd made a list in my journal of what I wanted in a man. I'd been determined to marry a Jew since I was eight years old. I also wanted someone who was kind, loving, good-humored, but also highly intelligent, well-educated, not clingy, but independent and able to enjoy life when alone as well as with people. Most importantly, someone who shared my Christian faith.

I joked that till now the only person who fulfilled every quality on my list was Jesus. I suddenly realized that Bob Isaacson indeed had every quality I'd listed and many more. Even better, he loved me. Many times, when I introduced him to friends, they would comment to me afterwards, "Do you know how madly in love with you that man is?"

This time I wholeheartedly consented to Bob's proposal, and we set our wedding date for June 1st, 1975. Bob called the realtor back. The realtor had good news. During our two week hold on the sale, the owner had dropped the price even further. Bob confirmed the sale. He also took me to meet his mother.

This was the first time I'd met any of Bob's family. He was the second-born of two sons. An attorney and school principal, his father had passed away five years before I met Bob. His entire family was highly educated and intellectual. I was thankful for all the years I'd worked hard to improve my own education so I could be a fitting partner for him.

I immediately fell in love with Bob's mother. She was not unlike me in personality, very self-sufficient and strong-willed, but also warm and friendly. Like the rest of her family, she was not religious, but she was very committed to Jewish tradition, and when she learned I wasn't Jewish, she became very upset. Though she didn't even attend synagogue, she went to the local rabbi to see what could be done to prevent her son marrying a Gentile Christian.

Like I said, she was a very strong-willed woman, and the shy, introverted Eleanor I'd been twenty years earlier could never have handled her. But at forty, I'd developed my own strength of will. Taking her out for lunch, I told her bluntly:

"Look, I know how upset you are that your Bobby is going to marry a non-Jewish wife. But I love your son very much. We are going to have a great life together, and we want you to be part of that life. I love you, and I don't want you to feel hurt by our wedding. To demonstrate that, we won't have our wedding inside a church. I know you feel that is disrespectful to your Jewish traditions. Instead, we are planning to have our wedding in a restaurant garden. The mayor of West Orange (a nearby town) will be marrying us. It will be just a small wedding, but very elegant and beautiful. I hope you understand I am doing this because I want you to be part of our lives."

"Oh, Eleanor, dah-ling!" she exclaimed in her characteristic New York drawl. Bob's mother was my ally from that moment. I became the daughter she'd never had. Mom Isaacson, as I called her, in turn became the mother I'd never had. In fact, if she felt my mother was being unkind to me, she'd tell her off.

"Eleanor is my child now!" she'd say.

Before the wedding, I took Bob up to meet Pop. By now Bob knew my history growing up in Germany and since. He was very protective of me, and on the way to Pop's house, he told me, "Now, Sweets, I don't like the way your father has been treating you all along. Your stepfather has been far more a father to you. So I'm going to make clear it will be your stepfather who walks you down the aisle at our wedding."

Arriving at Pop's house, we told them of our engagement. I showed them my beautiful engagement ring and invited them to the wedding. But from the moment we walked in, the atmosphere seemed strained. Were they upset about my engagement?

I'd chosen Johnny's birthday for our visit so I could bring him a present. Pop suggested we go out to a restaurant to celebrate. Once we'd ordered our meal, Pop raised a glass of wine to congratulate Johnny on his birthday. He didn't bother to even mention his daughter's engagement. I was used to Pop treating me like a casual acquaintance, so I ignored this, but I could see Bob was furious.

"I don't think they're happy you are getting married," he told me quietly.

It wasn't until Billie asked where we were going to live that I understood just what was happening. When I responded that Bob had just bought an eleven-room house in Short Hills, the atmosphere immediately chilled below freezing.

"Where in Short Hills?" Pop asked brusquely. "I have a side job cutting grass over there in the summer."

"The address is on Troy Drive," I explained. Pop looked furious. Then Billie spoke up. "I know that area. I go there once a month to do ironing for a lady who lives there."

I didn't know whether to laugh or cry as I realized Pop's fury was because he was jealous. I'd always been the rejected, unwanted daughter who crawled to him once a month for a polite visit he'd never reciprocated. Now God had blessed me, not just with a wonderful husband, but a beautiful home in a neighborhood where Pop could only aspire to be the gardener.

Billie spoke up thoughtfully, "You know, if you'll be living in Short Hills, you'll be wanting to hire someone to come in and clean."

Before she could suggest herself, Bob responded, "That won't be necessary. Eleanor will have a maid to do her cleaning."

Now both Pop and Billie looked as sour as a dill pickle. I must admit I couldn't help thinking of that Bible verse: "Vengeance is mine, says the Lord, "I will repay

(Deuteronomy 32:35)." Without my raising a single finger to bring it about, all their disdain and unkindness was being heaped back upon them.

Though at the time, I felt great embarrassment that my loving future husband should be witness to the way my father treated me. I needn't have worried. Bob understood good and well what was happening here, and he was already taking charge.

"Please know you are welcome to be at Eleanor's wedding," he told my father. "But I hope you understand that since her stepfather is the one who has given her a home and provided for her all these years, he will be the one walking her down the aisle."

I held my breath, not knowing whether Pop's temper might explode then and there. But he just kept his head down, looking at his hands, and made no response.

Our wedding was the following Sunday at 2 p.m. We'd invited only a dozen people, mainly because if we invited all my church and work friends and all Bob's family and colleagues, we'd need an entire cathedral. My church did give us a beautiful shower with lots of gifts. And for a full year after our wedding, Bob and I threw dinner parties for his friends and mine, gradually working our way through all the people we hadn't invited.

I was very happy with a small garden wedding. To me, marriage was a beautiful image of God bringing together husband and wife in sacred union. The very first wedding had been one man and one woman, Adam and Eve, in a beautiful garden, Eden, officiated by their Creator, God himself. So what could be better than to follow their example?

My only sadness was when Pop called the morning of the wedding to say he wouldn't be coming. His excuse was that Billie wasn't feeling well. I knew that wasn't the reason. Johnny did show up with his girlfriend. He handed Bob a check as wedding gift from Pop.

Furious on my behalf, Bob tore the check up, then wrote Pop a letter: "Eleanor doesn't need your money. She now has a loving husband to care for her needs. I am very disappointed in you that you couldn't show up at our wedding for even ten minutes after neglecting your daughter all her life. You should be ashamed at the way you have treated her. Until you apologize to her, you are not welcome in our home."

I learned from acquaintances of Pop that my father threw a temper tantrum when he received the letter. He never did apologize, and I had no further contact with Pop after that day. Saddened and embarrassed as I was that such a man could be my father, it was a relief not to deal with him again.

Meanwhile, I did not let Pop's snub spoil my joy. It was a wonderful day. The restaurant garden was decorated beautifully. I wore a dress of beautiful white lace and satin, topped off with a frothy lace hat instead of veil. Bob looked his most handsome, and I know we were both beaming radiantly. My heart was overflowing with love and joy as I repeated my vows: "I, Eleanor, take you, Robert, to be my wedded husband."

Of the entire day, one precious reality stood out. I'd been born Eleanor Drechsler. In all my life, my father's surname had meant nothing but loneliness, rejection, the assurance that I was unwanted. But that was now forever in my past. I had a new name. I was now Eleanor Isaacson, beloved wife of Dr. Robert Isaacson.

And with that new name, I could put the past behind me once and for all, focusing instead on the beautiful new life that lay before me with the man I loved. God had now indeed repaid to overflowing all the sad, lonely, silent years the locusts had eaten.

CHAPTER TWENTY-TWO

BELOVED

The Lord has anointed me . . . to comfort all who
mourn, and provide for those who grieve in Zion—to
bestow on them a crown of beauty instead of ashes,
the oil of joy instead of mourning, and a garment of
praise instead of a spirit of despair.

—Isaiah 61:1b-3a

Dear reader, I have now lived more than eight
decades on this earth. So I am qualified to say with
absolutely certainty that marriage to Dr. Robert
Isaacson was the most wonderful highlight of all my long life.
Our wedding ceremony was followed by an elegant dinner
with our guests. Once they'd all left, Bob and I lingered in the
restaurant garden.

Taking my hands in his, Bob made me a pledge: "Sweets,
I want you to understand that from this day forward, nobody,
but nobody—not your father nor your mother nor anyone
else—will ever be permitted to hurt you, neglect you, or
abandon you again. Not physically, mentally, or emotionally.
All that is over because you now have me to protect you and
love you. I will make it all up to you. All the pain, the

darkness, the starvation and suffering. The loneliness you endured as a motherless child. I will make it up to you a hundred-fold. And all the people who've hurt you will see it."

My sweet husband never broke that pledge. I told you earlier that I'd never found anyone but Jesus to fulfill the qualities I hoped for in a husband until I met Dr. Robert Isaacson. Conversely, I can say that the longer we were married, the more I saw the character of Christ evidenced in how Bob treated me. The Old Testament prophet Isaiah described how the coming Messiah would bring comfort to those who grieved, replace ashes with a crown of beauty, mourning with joy, despair with praise (Isaiah 61:1-4).

At a more human level, Bob did all that in my own life. Our Short Hills home was still being painted when we got married, so we took a honeymoon in the Poconos. But we kept it brief because we were both eager to settle into our new home together. We found a nearby church to attend and became active there. We did a lot of entertaining, inviting all our acquaintances over in turn. As couples do in a good marriage, we balanced each other out. I was the lively fireball, Bob the quiet, reserved scientist. But as time went on, he became the life of a party while I became less talkative.

As a child in war-torn Germany, God had given me a vision that I'd not only survive the bombs, but live to grow up to beautiful womanhood in a green valley of peace and plenty. That vision had now come to fruition. Bob insisted on treating me as his queen. He took me to concerts and Broadway shows, purchased subscriptions to the Lincoln Center and Carnegie Hall, bought me a new car along with far more clothes, furs, and jewelry than any one woman needed.

In fact, I learned not to voice any wishes too freely, as Bob would instantly rush out to indulge them. One day, I mentioned casually that I'd like to get blinds someday for the basement windows so no one could see me exercising when I was down there on my treadmill. Bob jumped to his feet and insisted on driving to Lowes that very minute. He'd take me to an exclusive boutique and have me model beautiful evening gowns. I'd glance discreetly at the price tags and insist on choosing the less expensive option. He'd pay the bill, then wait until we were home before handing me a shopping bag with the dress I'd chosen—along with the most expensive one I had modeled.

But it wasn't the material blessings I cared about. Bob made me feel loved every moment of every day. I in turn set a goal to make him as happy as he made me. I usually arrived home from work before Bob did, so I would quickly tidy my clothing and freshen my makeup. After all, if I could make such efforts for my employers, then why should I do less for my beloved husband? When he drove into the garage, I'd be standing at the door to meet him.

"Coming home to you is like emerging from the desert into a beautiful oasis," he'd tell me.

Bob still traveled a lot for Celanese—Germany, Japan, or shorter trips to North Carolina or California. So it was well I'd learned to be self-sufficient. I enjoyed life when he was home, but I could also enjoy myself when he was gone. He liked that I wasn't dependent on him to entertain myself.

Still, any time Bob could make it home, he did. One Sunday, all the Celanese managers flew to California for top management meetings scheduled all day Monday through Tuesday morning. After those meetings, they were scheduled to fly directly to Chicago for more meetings there on Wednesday. Bob called me after the Tuesday morning meetings had finished. "Sweets, I'm coming home. I'll be in this evening sometime."

"That's great!" I responded, surprised. "But don't you have to be in Chicago for meetings tomorrow? That is a lot of extra flying to come all the way home."

"I can catch an early morning flight to Chicago," he answered. "Spending a night home with you is worth the extra trip."

Was I loved, or what?

All this time, I was still working on my bachelor's degree. It wasn't long before Bob suggested I quit working so I could complete my degree. I did so. Attending college full time, I was able to finish within a year. In 1980, I graduated magna cum laude with a double degree in English and business management.

I immediately began looking for a new job. It wasn't that we couldn't live comfortably on Bob's income. But I liked staying busy and seeking new challenges. Bob's attitude about my returning to work was the same as it was about everything I did: "Whatever makes you happy makes me happy, Sweets!"

Remembering the advice of my psychology professor about my gift for sales, I found a job as an insurance agent for Mutual of Omaha. I remained at that job for ten years, and it indeed proved to be a position tailor-made for me. Within five years, I'd been voted #2 Female Agent for Mutual of Omaha in the entire United States. Since I was also still singing, speaking about my World War II experiences, and teaching Bible study, I stayed quite busy.

Bob expressed often how proud he was of me. As he'd pledged, Bob was also very protective of my emotional well-being. I continued to do my best to be a good, loving daughter to my mother. But Mom would often make unkind digs. By now, I'd been privileged to sing with New Jersey's famed Masterworks Chorus at both Lincoln Center and Carnegie Hall. Then one day, I was invited to be the soloist at a particularly prestigious concert.

"Why are they asking you?" Mom demanded. "You don't have the voice for something like that!"

As always, I did my best not to react. I never shared the things she said with Bob because I knew he'd get on the phone and chew her out. But he'd learned to read my expression. One April evening, he walked in with his usual greeting. "Hi, Sweets. How was your day?"

"Just fine," I responded.

He looked at me sharply, then placed both hands on my shoulders. "Okay, Sweets, what did your mother do today?"

"Nothing, really!" I insisted.

Leaving me, Bob went upstairs. When he came down, he was holding a gorgeous gold bracelet. "You know, Sweets, I think it's time for an early Christmas present."

That brought a smile, considering we were still in spring. Putting the bracelet on my wrist, Bob explained, "I buy presents throughout the year whenever I see something I think you will enjoy. So any time a problem reemerges from your childhood or someone treats you unkindly, you can expect me to pull out one of those presents just to show how much you are loved and that no one better dare hurt you when I'm around!"

When I graduated from college, Bob planned a celebratory dinner at a very exclusive restaurant. He'd invited both our mothers. Mom hated any event where she wasn't the center of attention, so she called to let me know she wasn't coming.

"Mom says she can't make it," I told Bob.

"She'll make it!" Bob responded firmly.

He got on the phone with my mother. I don't know what he said, but when we arrived at the celebratory dinner, she was there. Bob was no more tolerant of Mom mistreating me as of Pop, and he had no compunction about confronting her on it outside my presence. One might think this would make her angry. Instead, Mom came to have great respect for Bob and always behaved like a perfect angel around him.

In contrast to my own mother, Mom Isaacson had become a very dear friend. She lived ninety minutes from us, but spent one week a month at our home. I decorated a bedroom and bathroom as her own special suite. Though she'd come to accept her son marrying a Gentile Christian and even Bob's faith in Jesus as the Messiah, she'd made clear she didn't agree with our beliefs.

Still, when she stayed with us, Mom Isaacson insisted on accompanying me everywhere, including to church and the Bible studies I taught. When I made clear I didn't expect her to attend a Christian Bible study with me, she'd say with her New York drawl, "No, dah-ling, I just want to be with you."

During these years, I'd begun to battle allergies. We discovered that our house was infested with mold. So Bob suggested, "Sweets, I think we should design and build our own house."

We chose a new development right next to Short Hills called The Summit, where an exclusive community of just twenty-six custom-designed homes were being built. Bob and I had so much fun designing exactly what we wanted. Bob wanted a semi-circular driveway sweeping around the front like some fancy British manor house. I wanted a majestic entrance with tall, round columns leading to double-doors. Inside, an upstairs balcony looked down over a sunken living-room with a cathedral ceiling.

Bob designed his upstairs office, and I designed my own office right next to it with a bathroom in between. We created a special suite with private bath for my mother-in-law. A sunroom in the back opened onto a lush garden with flowers, trees, walkways, and a pagoda.

We moved in just in time for Christmas, 1985. It would be our dream home for the rest of our marriage. We were both so happy there, it would be hard to wish for more of life. Bob's mother loved coming to stay in her own special suite. Life was good.

But Mom Isaacson was becoming more frail. She'd been a widow for many years, and she was finding it increasingly difficult to live on her own, especially with us being ninety minutes away. Bob had an older brother, but he was not very active in either her life nor ours.

With Bob and I both working, the logical solution would be to find her a comfortable assisted living facility. But I wasn't happy with this decision. My own mother and stepfather were getting elderly too. It wouldn't be long before they also needed me to spend more time caring for them.

As usual, Bob expressed support of any decision I made. "You know, Sweets, if Mom moves in here, the biggest burden is going to fall on you. So whatever you decide is what we'll do."

Praying for wisdom, I came to the conclusion God was calling me to quit my job and dedicate myself to our aging parents. In 1990, I quit my job, and we moved Mom Isaacson into our home. It wasn't an easy adjustment. Except for finishing my college degree, I'd held a job continuously since my teens. Now I was staying home, doing the work of a domestic and nurse's aide. I can remember sitting at my desk in my upstairs office, wondering if I'd done the right thing. After all, if it didn't work out, I could hardly send my mother-in-law back to her apartment.

This is my turn to be a mother, I reminded myself. *Mom Isaacson has always been there for me. Whatever happens, I am going to commit myself to love and care for her.*

To my surprise, I discovered I didn't miss my job at all. In fact, I loved being a homemaker. Inviting friends over for lunch. Chauffeuring Mom Isaacson to doctor's appointments and on outings. I now had more time for entertaining, teaching Bible study, mentoring young women. Mom Isaacson attended church and Bible study with me, and while she never spoke about faith, she always bowed her head for prayer when Bob offered grace at meals.

I'd now entered a new season of life, one of restful tranquility, the rushing stream of my busy life quieted into still, calm waters. I had time to look back over my life with new perspective. My dark, painful childhood. My young adult years of silent withdrawal. The flowering of my beautiful womanhood. The glory of marriage to the love of my life.

I could see now the pattern God had been weaving from both the dark and light of my life journey. It brought to mind one of my favorite Bible verses:

And we know that in all things God works for the good of those who love him, who have been called according to his purpose.

—Romans 8:28)

Not only had God wrought his purpose from even my darkest hours, but for every dark moment, he'd blessed me with countless more of bright, glorious light. And God had used my beloved Bob as his instrument in blessing me.

That our Creator is sovereign and works all things for the good of his children was a truth I would soon need to cling to with all my strength.

Chapter Twenty-Three

Affliction's Furnace

I have tested you in the furnace of affliction.

—Isaiah 48:10b

I should make clear, dear reader, that our married lives had not been completely free of turmoil. Our first real crisis had been in 1979. We'd been married four years by then, and Bob was on a trip to Japan when I discovered a hard lump in one of my lymph nodes. I made a doctor's appointment the very next day. By the time Bob returned from Japan, I was undergoing a battery of tests, resulting in a diagnosis of cancer.

Bob was devastated at the news, but I found myself surprisingly calm. After all, this was hardly the first trial my life had held. If God could bring me through bombs, starvation, and deafness, he could bring me through cancer.

"Don't be upset," I consoled my husband. "This is just another test from the Lord. And believe me, it's nothing compared to all he's gotten me through so far!"

I went in for surgery. The doctors decided they'd gotten all the cancer, so I didn't have to do chemotherapy. But I did have to make changes in my lifestyle. As a good German, I loved my sausage, bacon, pot roasts, and other fatty meats. But when I learned about the connections between cancer remission and avoiding red meats, saturated fats, and other animal-based foods, I switched to a vegetarian diet. Believe me, this wasn't an easy sacrifice!

But it was worth it. For many years, my cancer stayed in remission. This experience even opened the doors to new opportunities for ministry, including another Bible study I began teaching. Of course, God could have chosen a very different outcome, and I was well aware of that. I had godly Christian friends who'd been diagnosed with cancer, but instead of healing them physically, God had taken them home to heaven.

What did I learn from this? I learned total dependence on God. This planet is not our home, and we are not here forever. When illness or any disaster strikes, we must learn to lean on God, both for his healing and for his sovereignty. In his perfect wisdom, God may choose to heal us, or he may be ready to call us home. We must trust that his choices for our lives are always those of a loving, caring heavenly Father who wants only the best for his children.

I would need to remind myself of those lessons as 1993 rolled around. One day as I was lying down, my arm became so painful I could hardly bear it. Running my fingers gingerly over the area, I discovered a new lump. Sure enough, when I went in for an examination, the doctors confirmed that my lymphoma had returned.

This time I had to undergo chemotherapy. I hope I am not vain, but it was hard to lose all my hair. My loving husband took a full day off work to shop with me for a wig. He helped me pick out a beautiful one. In fact, since we'd told few people about the resurgence of my cancer, I received many compliments about my beautifully groomed hair and slim figure. Not that I'd recommend cancer as a good dieting strategy!

I was happy to have Bob with me. We were looking forward to spending even more time together, since Bob had recently been offered a generous executive retirement package. Bob was only fifty-seven years old. But he'd grown tired of spending so much travel time away from me. With his brilliant mind and experience, he could set his own terms as a consultant. So he took the Celanese package, setting his retirement date for June, 1993, just after our anniversary.

Bob had never been particularly health conscious, not like I was, maintaining a strict vegetarian diet and regular exercise workouts. But since he spent so much of his day at a desk or in an airplane seat, we'd started taking long walks together every evening when he got home. Lately, each time we walked, his right shoulder would begin to hurt.

"Be thankful it's your right shoulder and not your left," I told him. "If it were your left, it could be a sign of a heart attack.".

Still, I was worried and suggested to Bob that he schedule a full physical. While his health had always been good, there had been one niggling concern since I had met him. On our very first formal date, he'd told me about his family, including his father who'd recently passed away.

"Dad was only fifty-seven when he died," he added. "I probably won't live beyond that age either."

Aghast, I'd responded, "Don't even say those words! You don't want to throw something like that out in the universe!"

By April, Bob hadn't gotten around to scheduling that physical. My own lymphoma was responding well to the chemo. It seemed that God had chosen to spare me once again. In celebration, Bob and I drove into New York City to attend a concert at Carnegie Hall. Classic New Yorkers, we drove into the city at least twice a month for events at the Lincoln Center or Carnegie Hall.

Or rather, I drove. Bob hated driving in New York as much as I loved it. Yes, I will admit I could be as aggressive as any New York taxi driver. Bob was secure enough in his masculinity he had no problem letting me drive, though he had a tendency to ride an imaginary brake pedal.

"Look, Sweets, a red light's coming!" he'd exclaim.

"It's a mile away! Just let me drive!" I'd respond. I think our only negative exchanges during our entire marriage were when I was driving and he in the passenger seat!

Bob being Bob, he'd reserved two of the best seats in Carnegie Hall. We were waiting for the concert when I looked over at my husband. A premonition swept over me as strong as the one that had propelled me past that first cave opening on Christmas, 1944. It whispered, *Take a look at Bob. This will be the last time you see him in this theater.*

Confused, I shook the odd feeling away, thinking, *Why? Are we going to drop our subscription to Carnegie?*

After the concert, we walked down to the parking garage. Once again, the premonition hit me. *Eleanor, this is the last time you'll see Bob walking down these steps.* Perplexed, I asked myself, *Where is he going?*

On the drive home, Bob brought up his retirement. "Just think, Sweets, six more weeks and I will be retired. No more trips away from you. I've been telling my colleagues that the best part of retirement is that I can be with my Sweets 24-7."

Now, dear reader, if you are married, no matter how much you love your spouse, you will understand the thoughts that flashed in my mind just then. I was braking for a red light, which allowed me to avoid an immediate answer. But I can be honest that overflowing delight wasn't the emotion running through my brain.

I thought of all my responsibilities teaching multiple Bible studies, mentoring and counseling women and young people, chauffeuring around Mom Isaacson as well as my own mother. *Okay, how am I going to handle this? Bob wants me 24-7. My mother-in-law wants me 24-7. God has called me to serve him 24-7. And I've been an independent person all my life. I kind of want me 24-7 too!*

Suddenly, that little voice of premonition said, *This isn't something you need to worry about. It will all work out, you'll see!*

The red light had given me time to organize my words. Aloud, I said, "You know, Bob. I can't see you just walking out of your office and doing nothing. It just isn't you. Maybe it would be good to have your consulting job in place before you retire. Maybe we can work on setting up your home office. Get new furnishing, stationery, business cards. It wouldn't hurt to even have some clients lined up in advance."

"I'll pray about it," was all Bob responded.

That was April. In early May, Bob finally scheduled his physical. His stress tests showed abnormal results, so the doctors scheduled a cardiac catheterization to check his heart. On Monday, May 17th, I checked him into a hospital room by 8 a.m. for the necessary preparatory procedures.

The catheterization itself was scheduled for 11 a.m. I'd been told Bob would be back from the catheterization by 2 p.m., so I returned then. But instead of being in recovery, Bob was still waiting in his original room.

I tracked down the nurse on duty. "What's going on?"

"His doctor's been called out of town," she told me. "We're waiting for another doctor to arrive to perform the procedure. He should be here any minute."

By 3 p.m., the doctor still hadn't showed. The expression on Bob's face made clear he was ready to just walk out of the hospital and forget the procedure altogether. By evening, a doctor finally showed up and performed the procedure. When I returned the next morning to take Bob home, the doctor informed us that the catheterization had revealed four clogged arteries. Bob would need to undergo an angioplasty, which is a procedure where a tiny balloon is inserted into the artery to clear the obstruction, not unlike clearing out a plugged drain pipe. The angioplasty had already been scheduled for a date two weeks away.

"Why are you waiting two weeks?" I demanded anxiously. "If he has clogged arteries, why isn't he on the operating table right now?"

"It's protocol," the doctor assured me. "In the meantime, Bob needs to follow a strict vegetarian diet, at least until the procedure."

That wouldn't be an issue, since I'd been cooking vegetarian for myself for years. Bob wasn't happy, since he enjoyed fine dining. But he agreed to follow the doctor's instructions. That was Tuesday.

On Wednesday evening, Bob and I had both already showered and were in our pajamas ready for bed, when a young woman I was mentoring called. I was on the phone with her, talking through some of her marital difficulties, when I heard Bob calling out for me. "Sweets, I'm having chest pains!"

I broke off the phone call and went to him. "Let's get you out of these pajamas and to the emergency room!"

When we reached the hospital, the doctors immediately admitted Bob into the intensive care unit while I filled out paperwork. One of the doctors asked me, "Has your husband ever had any problems with bleeding? Nose bleeds? Cuts that wouldn't heal?"

The questions were because they wanted to administer a TPA injection. TPA, or tissue plasminogen activator, is a commonly prescribed drug for stroke or heart attacks, since both conditions are often caused by blood clots, and TPA can help break up and dissolve the clot. Of course, the very factors that allow TPA to dissolve a blood clot put the patient at risk for bleeding, since the blood's ability to clot quickly is compromised.

I knew about this drug because Bob had been part of the team that spearheaded research and marketing for TPA. It was considered a miracle drug for heart patients. We signed the medical release form stating that Bob had no known issues of nose bleeds or other such symptoms. Bob was quite cheerful as a nurse set up an intravenous feed to administer the TPA.

"I can't believe I'm getting the benefit of a drug I developed marketing for," he commented with a smile. He went into great detail, telling them all about the benefits and low risks of TPA. The risks included minor bleeding in the gums or nose for about 25% of patients. There was also some danger of a cerebral hemorrhage, but in only 1% of patients, and the doctors would be monitoring for that. So while we were both concerned about his chest pains, we felt no concern at all about possible side effects.

I stayed with Bob until 2 a.m., then had to leave since I'd left Mom Isaacson at home alone. The next morning, I drove Mom Isaacson to visit Bob. I asked her to wait in the lobby while I headed to ICU to check on him first. When I entered his room, I was stunned to find Bob crying. It was so out of character for my calm, reserved scientist husband.

"What's the matter?" I asked anxiously.

His face wet with tears, he answered sorrowfully, "I'm going to die and leave you, Sweets."

Taking his hand, I kissed him. "What are you talking about? You're looking so much better. They prevented a heart attack with the drug you developed. How can you say this?"

Returning to the lobby, I brought Mom Isaacson up to visit. We sat down on opposite sides of Bob's hospital bed. Bob reached out to take my hand in one of his, then reached out the other to take his mother's hand. Looking at his mother, he said, "Please take care of my Sweets for me."

Then Bob turned his head to give me a loving look. "Sweets, please take care of Mom. You need each other now."

That he was saying goodbye to both of us went right over my head. The afternoon was wearing on. At 3:30 p.m., I stood up. "Bob, let me go home and give Mom her supper. Then I'll come back. Is there anything you'd like me to bring you?"

"Sure, my reading glasses," he responded. "And maybe today's paper and a book to read."

"Okay, I'll do that." Mom Isaacson and I left. I popped into the hospital drugstore to buy the day's paper, then took Mom Isaacson home and prepared supper. After we'd eaten, I gathered the items Bob had requested. But before I could leave, Mom Isaacson grabbed her coat.

"I don't want you going back there all alone," she insisted. So we drove back to the hospital together. As soon as we walked into ICU, a doctor met us.

"There's been a major turn of events," he informed us. It turned out that my Bob fell into the 1% of TPA recipients in whom the drug triggered a cerebral hemorrhage. He'd suffered major bleeding in the brain not long after we'd left, and now he was unconscious. "We've already called the specialist and have an operating room scheduled."

Bob was wheeled into the operating room. I called our church and the women from my Bible studies, asking for prayer. Soon, the waiting room was filled with friends who'd come to be with me. Together, we prayed and waited and prayed and waited. Around ten p.m., the brain surgeon walked in, looking exhausted.

"We've cleaned up the hemorrhage," he told me. "But that's all we could do. If Bob is to recover consciousness, it will take a miracle."

"We'll have a miracle," I responded confidently. "All of us here have been praying. We have a God who opened the Red Sea. He can heal my Bob."

"Yes, wonderful!" the doctor mumbled, looking far from convinced.

The next day, I was at Bob's bedside bright and early. Holding his hand in mine, I pleaded, "Bob, if you can hear me, please squeeze my hand."

To my relief, Bob's hand closed weakly on mine. Maybe he couldn't speak, but I knew my wonderful husband was in that supine, silent frame hooked up like some machine to countless tubes and wires. All day, I sat there, gently squeezing Bob's hand and talking to him. He would occasionally squeeze my hand back, so I knew he was listening.

As I talked to Bob, I also spoke to my heavenly Father. *Dear Lord, this is the only real trial my husband has faced since coming to know Yeshua as Lord and Savior. I know this will strengthen his faith, as my own trials have strengthened mine.*

I went home that night feeling optimistic. But the next morning, the phone was ringing by 7:30 a.m. It was the hospital. When I spoke to Bob's surgeon, he had more bad news. "Mrs. Isaacson, your husband has suffered another extensive brain hemorrhage. We're taking him to surgery now to clean up the damage. But I have to be honest with you. I've been a brain surgeon for fifteen years, and I've never known anyone to survive two such hemorrhages."

"I don't want to hear that!" I told him sharply. "God can heal my husband."

"Yes, that's possible," the surgeon admitted. "But it isn't likely. And if he does survive, he will be a vegetable with all brain function gone."

Bob survived the surgery, but he never recovered consciousness. For the next four months, he remained in a coma. During this entire period, I was also facing my own battle with cancer. I still hadn't shared with anyone that my lymphoma was back, so I tried to hide just how exhausted the chemo left me. It had also left me completely bald, so I couldn't go anywhere without a wig. One day I encountered a woman who with her husband were good friends of Bob and me. She exclaimed over how well I was looking.

"You know, my husband and I really admire you, Eleanor," she went on. "Here you are with Bob in a coma. And yet every time you step out of the house, you are elegantly dressed with not a hair out of place. And those beautiful headbands and hats with the bow tilted at the perfect angle just like a model on the runway. I was telling my husband, thank God she's keeping up appearances for fashion and not illness."

Something in my expression must have sunk in because she broke off to look at me sharply. "That *is* it, isn't it, Eleanor? I mean, it *is* for fashion, not illness!"

I managed to smile. "Well, actually, no."

"Oh, no! Please don't tell me you're on chemo!" She burst into tears. "I don't understand how you do it, Eleanor! How can you possibly stay so positive going through cancer at the same time you're having to watch your husband die?"

The Bible tells us to always be ready with an answer for those who ask about the hope we have in us (1 Peter 3:15). However I might feel inside, I knew the answer and gave it unhesitatingly. "I can tell you how I do it. It is because I have a relationship with Jesus Christ. What is the worst that can happen? If I die, I will go to be with my Savior. In the meantime, he gives me the strength and courage to move forward. Like the Bible tells us in Psalm 46:1, God is my refuge and strength. He is my ever-present help in times of trouble. So I have no need to fear, though the earth shake and the mountains fall into the sea."

By September, life had become a routine of visiting an unresponsive Bob, my own medical appointments, caring for

Mom Isaacson, and trying to juggle all other aspects of daily life in between. One day in early September, a dear friend from one of my Bible studies named Maria said to me, "Eleanor, you are going to have to face that your Bob isn't going to make it. I don't want you left to cope with everything after he stops breathing. Especially since you'll be dealing with your mother-in-law as well. Why don't you let me help you get all the arrangements in place now. If you end up not needing them, so much the better. But at least you'll be prepared."

I knew Maria was right. I'd already come to realized what a blessing it was that we'd moved Mom Isaacson in when we did. I don't know what she'd have done if Bob had fallen ill when she was still in her apartment ninety minutes away. For my part, it was a comfort and relief not to be alone in the big house that had been such a warm, inviting home when Bob was in it. With just the two of us, Mom Isaacson and I became even closer. My Bible study friends teasingly called us Naomi and Ruth, after the famed daughter-in-law/mother-in-law pair in the Old Testament book of Ruth.

With Maria's help, I went to a funeral home and made all the necessary arrangements. I picked out Bob's favorite outfit—a blue suit, white shirt, red tie, socks, and shoes. I talked to a Messianic rabbi about officiating the funeral, since I wanted the service to honor Bob's Jewish heritage as well as his faith in Jesus as Messiah. With preparations complete, I went back to the hospital.

I sat beside Bob's bed, holding his hand and talking to him. He had some color in his face and to my eyes actually seemed somewhat better. I lifted my thoughts heavenward. *Okay, God, now that I've made the arrangements, I'll bet Bob is going to wake up. He's going to walk out of here and come home with me.*

One of the nurses I'd come to recognize over the months of visiting approached me. With gentleness, she said, "Mrs. Isaacson, you have wonderful faith. I've heard a lot about people having faith, but I'd never really seen it firsthand. I've definitely seen it in you. It is so refreshing. But I want you to be realistic. Your husband isn't going to wake up. We've stopped all coma patient therapy because right now he is just hanging on. What we need now from you is a Do Not Resuscitate order. Otherwise, when he finally lets go, we're going to have to bring in all kinds of machines that will just be to maintain his body functions even though he will be gone."

When I went home that evening, it felt like the worst day of my life. My precious husband's life was now in my hands.

No, it isn't! I realized. Tears streaming down my cheeks, I began to pray. *Dear God, I've trusted you to work good in everything that has come into my life, the dark and the light, the good and the bad. If you choose to take my Bob home now, I know you have your reasons. I was single for so many years before I met Bob. If you choose to leave me single again now, I will trust it is your will for me and for Bob. And I will continue to serve you with my life, married or single.*

I went back to the hospital and signed a Do Not Resuscitate order. All the doctors assured me I'd made the right decision. But once it was signed, I broke down. Every time someone stopped by to visit, I would throw my arms around them and burst into tears.

By Thursday, I had no tears left. When I got up that morning, I said to Mom Isaacson, "I'm not feeling well. I've been at the hospital all day every day. Instead of going in for the 11 a.m. visiting period, let's wait till the 3 p.m. period."

We rested for the remainder of the morning. But when I called around noon, the nurse on duty told me, "Eleanor, you need to get here as soon as possible. He's just waiting for you to be here."

Mom Isaacson and I rushed to the hospital. When we got there, I found Bob gasping for air. I knew he couldn't hear me, but I put my arms around him, kissed him, then rested my forehead against his. I'd wished so much to hear my sweet Bob speak again. I knew now that his last charge to his mother and me would be the final words I'd hear him speak.

Raising my head, I saw one of the doctors, the husband of a young woman I mentored. I knew he wasn't scheduled to be on duty that day, so I asked him, "Morris, what are you doing here?"

"I just had to come in to be with you," he said. "You must know it isn't looking good."

"I know," I responded.

I sat there for another two hours. Bob's breathing was increasingly labored. Then all was suddenly quiet. At 5:30 p.m., on Thursday, September 16, 1993, my wonderful husband, the love of my life, Dr. Robert Isaacson, left my side and stepped into the presence of his Messiah and Savior, Jesus Christ. He was 57 years old, the same age at which his father had passed away.

Dearest reader, by now you know that I make a spiritual application to everything that happens in my life. 5:30 p.m. was the time Bob drove into the garage each evening and stepped into my kitchen, calling joyously, "Sweets, I'm home!"

As I sat there, my tear-filled eyes on my husband's still face, I lifted my heart and words to my heavenly Father. *Dear God, for eighteen years Bob's went walking in to greet me at this exact hour. Today he didn't walk into my house. But he's walked into yours, and I know he is with you right now.*

A passage I'd taught often to others in my Bible studies rose to my mind:

> But I do not want you to be ignorant, brethren, concerning those who have fallen asleep, lest you sorrow as others who have no hope. For if we believe that Jesus died and rose again, even so God will bring with Him those who sleep in Jesus . . . And thus we shall always be with the Lord. Therefore comfort one another with these words.
>
> —1 Thessalonians 4:13-18

Today it was I who drew comfort from that sweet promise. My Bob had not left me. He'd simply gone on ahead. It might be a short wait or a long one. But in God's time, I would see my beloved husband again in Glory with all others who are part of God's great family.

Dear reader, that was almost twenty-five years ago, and I am still waiting. Which simply means that God's purpose for me this side of heaven is not yet complete!

CHAPTER TWENTY-FOUR

PRESSING FORWARD

"For my thoughts are not your thoughts, neither are your ways my ways," declares the LORD. "As the heavens are higher than the earth, so are my ways higher than your ways and my thoughts than your thoughts."

—Isaiah 55:8-9

So I entered a new season in my life—widowhood. It was now that the years of learning total dependence on God came to fruition. More than two hundred friends and work colleagues attended Bob's funeral. The service officiated by a Messianic Jewish rabbi offered a deeply inspirational message of comfort and hope. The eulogies were a wonderful tribute to my Bob. But I went through the day in a haze of exhaustion, not just from the chemo, but from my grief.

Still, I knew I needed to move forward. I also needed to be there for Mom Isaacson, who was also grieving the death of her son. Standing beside that closed casket as it was lowered into its final resting place, I reminded myself, *There lies the dearest person I have ever loved. But there also lies the will of God for my life. Bob's work here on this earth is complete, so God took him home. I am still here, so mine isn't done. Now that God has called me once again to be single, I need to find out what he wants me to do next.*

My own mother was in attendance at the funeral. But it proved too much to hope Mom might get through even such an occasion as this without making a scene. We'd planned a luncheon to follow the funeral. It was by invitation only, but we let Mom know in advance she was welcome to join us. Despite this, Mom showed up with some friend neither I nor Bob's mother had ever met and insisted on bringing her to the luncheon.

I've mentioned before that Mom Isaacson was a strong-minded woman, much like me, who didn't take to being pushed around. She told my mother in no uncertain terms that extra guests, above all, total strangers, were not welcome at the luncheon. Mom came to me, furious. "How dare she treat me like this? Why shouldn't I bring a guest if I choose?"

I had neither strength nor patience for a battle with my mother on this of all days. Flatly, I told her, "Mom, this isn't about you! Pauline [Mom Isaacson's given name] just buried her son today. If she doesn't want strangers around, that is her choice."

Unconvinced, Mom flounced indignantly away. My mother-in-law and I returned home to pick up the threads of our daily lives. Every new "first" brought fresh grief. Sitting down to dinner without Bob. Attending church alone. Even finishing my chemo. The treatments had worked, and the doctors told me I was in complete remission. The irony seemed senseless. Here I'd gone through two bouts of cancer, and yet I was once again looking forward to many years of life ahead, while my Bob, who'd hardly known a day of sickness, was gone at the young age of fifty-seven.

God's ways are not our ways, nor his thoughts our thoughts, I reminded myself. *It doesn't have to make sense to me, because I know it does make sense to God, and he has a loving, caring purpose for even this that will be for my ultimate good.*

Cleaning out Bob's personal effects was another difficult experience. Unable to sleep, I went into his closet one night at 2 a.m. and began neatly folding all his clothing into bags to take to Good Will. But when I'd finished, the shelves and hangers looked so unfamiliar in their bareness I started to cry. Dumping out the freshly packed clothing, I hung it all back up in the closet.

Christmas and New Year's were especially hard. Bob had been my only real family. Once again, I felt grateful to have my mother-in-law with me. Caring for her was a welcome distraction from wallowing in my own grief. Like the biblical Naomi and Ruth, we became even closer now that we had only each other.

One thing Bob and I had done each New Year was to write out a list of what we'd accomplished in the past year, then set a new goal together for the coming year. It might be something practical like necessary house repairs or something personal we wanted to achieve. This year, I sat alone in the bedroom Bob and I had shared, writing out a list on my own. My husband had been gone now for three months. I would never love him less, but I also knew I couldn't keep dwelling on the past. And that included the home we'd built together.

God, I can't just sit here looking at the chair where Bob had his chest pains, I prayed. *Or all the other things that hold memories of Bob. If you are calling me to widowhood, then please help me make it a glorious widowhood, as glorious as my marriage to Bob.*

For a first step, I decided that my New Year's goal would be a complete redecoration of the house. By the end of New Year's Day, I'd rearranged my bedroom, including moving Bob's chair to a new location. On January 2nd, I began calling contractors to choose new wall paper, paint, carpets, etc. By the end of January, the entire house was rearranged and redecorated.

From that point on, I made a conscious choice to pull out all the stops in living widowhood to the full. Above all, I wanted my life to be a help and example to others who were facing loneliness, rejection, grief. I began teaching a Bible study for widows. In fact, I was now teaching a different Bible study almost every day. I also continued the mentoring and counseling ministry I'd begun during my marriage to young married women as well as divorced and single moms. My home became a haven to the lonely, and many times women would just stay over because we'd talked so late into the night.

One group who attended my Bible studies stands out, the Mother Superior and some other nuns from a nearby convent. They came for over a year and always took copious notes. One nun, Sister Elaine, would sleep over at my house after the Bible study just because she had so many questions to ask, and I didn't like her driving home late at night. When we got up in the morning, she'd have more questions to ask before heading back to the convent.

One day, I asked Sister Elaine, "How is it that you all keep coming to my Bible study, considering I'm a Protestant and you are all Catholic?"

I was surprised at her response. "Well, you see, Eleanor, we have a Pope now who has advised us to go to you Protestants to learn the Bible."

That was Pope John Paul II, the Polish pope who was an underground seminary student during the Nazi occupation and whose work in helping Polish Jews escape the Nazis was honored by the State of Israel. Among the many changes he'd effected in the Catholic Church had indeed been a new emphasis on both clergy and ordinary church members reading and studying the Bible for themselves instead of leaving it to the priesthood.

This Bible study led to the Mother Superior inviting me to speak about my WWII experiences at the convent. She'd invited another convent as well, so I found myself standing in front of a hundred-plus nuns, all dressed in black. After that, I was invited to visit the convent once a month, during which I would share with the nuns a short message from the Bible.

Nor did I neglect the friends and associates Bob and I socialized with before his death. I held a dinner party for our entire community of twenty-six houses. Neighbors I'd never even met came, and the party was such a success, I began holding them once a month. I hosted a concert in our beautiful garden as a fundraiser for the New Jersey symphony. I continued to speak at countless secular and church events.

Another ministry actually grew out of a business I started long before I even married Bob. When I worked as Director of Admissions and Instructor at Barbizon School of Modeling, I taught women the same skills that transformed my life—social graces, hair and skin care, wardrobe planning, etc. Once I began mentoring and counseling other women, I found that many of them needed help with their outer presentation as well as inner spiritual life. So I founded Image Dynamics, which combined Bible teaching and spiritual development with practical skills like beauty and wardrobe consulting, public speaking, proper diet and exercise habits. The tagline on my business cards read: "Be the best you can be from the inside out."

Whenever I shared my war experiences, whether in a secular or church environment, I always shared as well the miracle of God saving my life as well as my faith in God. Likewise, when I taught personal development skills. That said, I've never pushed my faith on anyone. Those I've seen come to faith in Jesus Christ do so because they've witnessed the change my faith has made in my own life and they want that change in their lives too.

One woman in particular came into my life because someone gave her one of my business cards at a conference. When Barbara called me, I asked her what had led her to seek me out.

"Well, I've had cancer, and my mother recently passed away," she explained. "We had a very difficult relationship, and it's been very stressful. My health is suffering, so I'd like to learn how to eat and exercise better."

As we chatted, I mentioned that my own husband had passed away just one year ago. Barbara responded emotionally, "How can you sound so positive? I still am so very angry inside at the way my mother treated me. How do you do it?"

"It's my faith that keeps me going," I responded. "Look, if you aren't doing anything right now, why don't you hop in your car and come up here. I'll make dinner, and we can talk."

Barbara was silent a moment. "You'd invite me to your house when you don't even know me?"

"Sure, why not?"

Ninety minutes later, Barbara was at my door with a bouquet of flowers. Mom Isaacson was with me as usual, and we sat down to dinner, my mother-in-law and I bowed our heads to say grace. Barbara bowed her head as well. While we ate, I asked discreetly about her background.

"I'm Jewish," she said. "Though not really religious."

"Really! My husband was Jewish too," I answered. "He wasn't religious either until he came to know Yeshua, the rejected Messiah of Israel. It's because of my faith in Yeshua that I can be positive and joyful, no matter what comes into my life. Yeshua is the way, the truth, and the life (John 14:6). When you know him, you have access to God, and you have connection to all his strength, love, hope."

"I want that too!" Barbara exclaimed.

She came over for dinner regularly after that. She would tell me all about her life, issues with her family, and her mother's death. I, in turn, shared with her what the Jewish Torah (Old Testament) had to say about the Messiah and how those teachings found fulfillment in the New Testament. On Monday evening, January 16, 1995, she bowed her head and invited Yeshua into her life. For years after, we studied the

Bible together, and though we no longer live nearby, to this day, Barbara remains one of my dearest friends.

Two other losses came into my life during this season. My mother-in-law had been growing steadily frail and clouded of mind since losing Bob. She still loved to go with me everywhere she could, including my Bible studies and other speaking engagements. But within three years of Bob's death, she became too weak to leave her bed.

In all these years, Mom Isaacson had never really said what she thought about my teaching. But one day as I was visiting at her bedside, she said in her loving New York drawl, "You know, Eleanor dah-ling, I've been watching you all these years. You've always had such peace and joy. I want what you have. I want to believe like you do."

That day, I was able to lead Mom Isaacson to a clear expression of faith in Yeshua as her Messiah. A few weeks later, she had the precious privilege of going ahead of me to see our beloved Bob again. She was eighty-nine years old.

It was shortly after Mom's Isaacson's death that I traveled to Bibletown in Boca Raton, Florida, where God revealed to me the vision I'd been given as a ten-year-old running from machine gun in Plauen. For the next decade, I traveled down there to enjoy that tranquil, green paradise and the fellowship of other Christians until I finally sold the condo in 2006.

Saying goodbye to Mom Isaacson had been another emotional experience. My stepfather's death was less distressing, but painful in its own way. Otto Steimle and I had not enjoyed a good relationship. While he'd fed and housed me for many years, he'd been as unkind to me in his own way as both my parents. He'd also treated me as a father shouldn't treat a teenage daughter, never so far as sexual assault, but perilously close, one reason I'd been so happy to move out into my own apartment. As with so much else in my life, Mom had ignored his actions or, if I brought them to her attention, blamed them on my "flirtatious" ways.

Our relationship improved somewhat when he came to know Christ as his Savior just a few years before he died. But I never felt comfortable in his presence. Mom had left all the arrangements for his funeral to me, so I found myself driving alone to meet with the funeral home director. At least I had peace Otto was now in heaven. But terrible memories of how he'd treated me kept surfacing so that when I reached the funeral home, I just couldn't get out of the car.

As I sat there, trying to regain my composure, I lifted up a desperate prayer to my true and only Father. *Dear God, you know how unpleasant all this is for me. I know I'm supposed to live by faith, no matter what comes my way. But I really need you in a special way today as I walk in there to sign all those papers. Won't you please show yourself to me?*

I felt immediate peace that God would answer my prayer. I don't know exactly what I was expecting. Maybe that an angel would walk right through the funeral home wall or window. Instead, as I walked into the funeral director's office, my eye fell on an ashtray sitting on his desk. He must have been of Jewish heritage, since the ashtray was emblazoned with a six-pointed Star of David.

The Star of David had fascinated me since I'd stepped out of that bakery as a little girl and seen two thin, worn-faced men with a bright-gold Star of David on their sleeves cleaning snow and ice from the sidewalks. I'd tried to find an explanation for what the six-pointed star meant. When I'd married a Jewish husband, I'd asked him, but he had no idea except that it was tradition. An orthodox rabbi had shrugged when I asked him. "I don't know. It's just mystical."

So I'd turned to the only true source of wisdom, praying that God himself would show me what it meant. One day I was reading the New Testament book of Hebrews. In chapter thirteen, verse five, one phrase jumped out at me:

> God has said, "Never will I leave you; never will I forsake you."

Somehow with those words, illumination filled my mind. The six points of the Star of David was formed by two intersecting triangles, one triangle pointing upward, the other pointing downward Such triangles were common symbolism for a trinity. The trinity of God himself—God, the Father, God the Son, God, the Holy Spirit. But also the trinity of humankind created in God's image—body, soul, and spirit.

God, the Trinity, had given his unbreakable promise to his people, the nation of Israel, and all others who placed their faith in God, that he would never leave us or forsake us. The intersected trinities of the Star of David was a perfect symbol of that promise. The trinity of man's body, soul, and spirit looking upward towards God. The trinity of Father, Son, and Holy Spirit looking downward towards God's children. And both trinities intrinsically connected for all eternity, because however short God's children might fall, God in his faithfulness and immeasurable love will never abandon us.

All that went through my mind as I looked at that ash tray, and I knew God was showing himself to me in a very personal, special way at that moment. This was my Lord's way of telling me, "Eleanor, I'm here. I'm connected with you and abiding in you. You will never be alone."

Chapter Twenty-Five

A Time to Dance

You have turned for me my mourning into dancing;
you have put off my sackcloth and clothed me with
gladness, to the end that my glory may sing praise
to You and not be silent. O LORD my God, I will give
thanks to You forever.

—Psalm 30:11-12

M y Bob had been gone seven years when dancing
entered my life.

Let me explain, dear reader, why this is
significant. As you might imagine, my childhood years in
war-torn Germany hardly offered cause for such
celebrations. When I came to America, the shy, withdrawn
loner I was did not attract invitations to proms, school
dances, or parties.

Then came the deaf years when music only existed as
echoed memories in my mind. Besides, if a burgundy-red
coat or lip gloss constituted worldliness, my spiritual mentor,
Marian, had taught me well that dancing or any joyous
movement of the body was disgraceful, if not outright sin. My

outward metamorphosis had not included dancing, and once I met Bob, our social outlets ran to concerts and theater, not a dance floor.

So how did a complete novice at the age of sixty-six find herself, not just on a dance floor, but entering the world of competitive ballroom dance? It began with my commitment to stay fit and healthy, regardless of my inner emotion. Counselors talk about the five stages of grief—denial, anger, guilt, depression, acceptance. It's easy to allow inner emotions like anger, guilt, depression to pull us physically into a downward spiral.

Conversely, a healthy lifestyle helps the mind process grief more productively. I'd had a health club membership for years, but found myself bored with the fitness routines. And while I'd moved forward, I still missed Bob. In general, I could keep my grief pushed down. Then I would be at a concert or some other activity Bob and I enjoyed together, and his absence would sweep over me so that I could barely breathe. I was looking for a new hobby that would not only keep me fit, but so busy I didn't have time to mourn.

One day I returned home from the health club. With Mom Isaacson now gone too, my big house echoed with emptiness. Turning on the TV, I sat there alone, channel surfing. I paused on a program featuring a Russian couple who were elegantly dressed, but also perspiring and very physically fit. Listening to the commentator, I realized they were waiting for a judge panel to announce their score. With their beautiful costumes, maybe they were ice-skaters.

As I kept watching, I discovered they weren't skaters, but competitive ballroom dancers. The next couple took the floor, dancing a waltz, the female dancer's brightly-hued skirt swirling around her. How beautiful they looked! And what a wonderful way to exercise!

Then all possible objections flooded my mind. *Eleanor, you don't even know how to dance! Besides, remember what Marian always said. A good Christian doesn't so much as think the word "dance"! What would your church friends say if you even considered such an activity?*

Then the same rebellion I'd felt when Marian criticized my burgundy-red coat rose up inside me. Why was I still worrying about what other people thought? The only true judge of my behavior was God. And by this point, I'd learned there was a big difference between what God actually said in his Word and what religious authorities chose to impose upon their followers. Opening my Bible, I decided to investigate what God had to say about dancing. I read King David's passionate thanksgiving to God:

> You turned my wailing into *dancing* . . . that my
> heart may sing your praises and not be silent.
>
> —Psalm 30:11-12a, NIV

I read the instructions given to Israel for their times of worship:

> Sing to the LORD a new song, his praise in the
> assembly of his faithful people . . . Let them praise
> his name with *dancing* and make music to him with
> timbrel and harp.
>
> —Psalm 149:1-3

> Praise God in his sanctuary . . .Praise him with the
> sounding of the trumpet, praise him with the harp
> and lyre, praise him with timbrel and *dancing*,
> praise him with the strings and pipe, praise him
> with the clash of cymbals, praise him with
> resounding cymbals.
>
> —Psalm 150:1b-5

The scripture verses evoked an image of those whirling ballroom dancers with a full orchestra playing in the background. Certainly nothing like the condemnation of dance I'd always been taught. I went on to read about the Israelite women dancing with their tambourines in praise for God's deliverance from Egypt (Exodus 15:20). King David dancing with all his might before the Lord as the Ark of the Covenant was brought home to Jerusalem (2 Samuel 6:14-15). The prophet Jeremiah's beautiful promise from God of a repentant Israel dancing for joy when God brought them home from captivity (Jeremiah 31:40.). Then I read a passage that struck a deep chord in my heart:

> There is a time for everything, and a season for every
> activity under the heavens: a time to be born and a
> time to die . . . a time to weep and a time to laugh,
> a time to mourn and a time to *dance*.
>
> —Ecclesiastes 3:1-4

I knew immediately that this was God's personal message to me. With God's mercy and love, I had endured this difficult season of weeping and mourning the death of my beloved husband. Now it was time for a new season of restored joy and laughter. Yes, and for dancing.

I never doubted from that moment that God had given his blessing on this new activity in my life. Still, I prayed, as I'd prayed so often before, *God, if you want me to pursue this, please make it clear by opening the way for me. First, there must be people in this community of ballroom dancing who are seeking after you. Second, I don't want to do this just for my own pleasure. Let there be young people, even foreigners like that Russian couple, who need a friend like me to share your love with them.*

This was September, 2000. Sometime earlier at a symphony fundraiser I was hosting, I'd met a female physician who'd immigrated from Czechoslovakia. As we chatted, I told her I was from Germany, but that in my childhood during the Russian occupation, I'd crossed the Czech border as a smuggler. We exchanged contact information, and she later called to invite me to Christmas dinner.

I was helping my hostess carry the dessert course from the kitchen when I noticed a wall bracket with a half-dozen medallions on ribbons hanging from it. Her entire Slovakian holiday feast had been delicious, so I gestured jokingly to the medallions. "Are those from a bake competition?"

She smiled. "Oh, no! I'm a competitive ballroom dancer. You really should give it a try. It's the most wonderful exercise for staying fit."

Well! I had asked God to give me clear direction, and once again, he couldn't have made it clearer. "Wow! Please, tell me all about it."

We ended up discussing the topic so long someone came to find out why we'd never delivered the dessert course. That ended our discussion, but as we carried out cake and hot drinks, she said, "Listen, my dance teacher was a surgeon back in Moscow. But he can't practice here, so he has opened six dance studios. One of them isn't far from you. Why don't you call him up after the holidays and tell him I sent you. You'll get one free lesson, which will let you see if it's something you'd enjoy."

"Sure, I'd love to do that." I took down the information, and as soon as the holidays were over, I made my appointment for a free lesson. The dance studio was on the fifth floor of an old building just ten minutes from my home. I was wearing three-inch heels, and as I started up the five flights of stairs, I prayed, *Okay, God, it sure seems you are bringing this into my life. But if you want me to do this, please make it very plain. If I do well this first time, I will take it as from you that I need to do this. But if anything negative happens, if I trip on these stairs or the dance floor, if I make a total fool of myself in the lesson, I'll take it as your direction not to do this.*

The husband and wife team who opened the studio door were both Russian, dressed beautifully for a ballroom floor. I still remembered some of the Russian I'd learned in school, so we chatted briefly in my limited Russian and their much better English. Then the instructor said, "Okay, let's start your lesson. What would you like to dance?"

"Well, I've never actually danced anything before," I admitted.

He tugged on his beard, looking surprised. "Hmm. Then what is your favorite style of music?"

"The Viennese Waltz," I told him.

Surprise turned to hesitancy. "That is the most difficult dance form we teach here. We don't normally ever start anyone on that."

I was actually pleased to hear this. I breathed a quick prayer. *Okay, God, this is good because if I do well, I will know it must be a sign from you.*

The instructor spoke to his wife in Russian. She pushed a button, and a waltz began playing. Then he turned back to me. "Now, you don't need to do anything, just follow me."

You don't need to do anything, just follow me! That is a message from God too! Following the instructor's lead, I kept up easily as we waltzed around the vast hardwood floor. Not once did I trip in my three-inch heels. When we'd returned to our starting place, the instructor asked, "Are you sure you've never danced before? This is our most difficult dance, and you did it amazingly well if this is your first time."

"Well, I'm German, and I grew up on Johann Strauss," I responded with a smile. "Maybe that's it."

"No, you have a natural talent," he responded. "I'd love to teach you. I recommend we start with two lessons a week."

Driving home, I prayed, *Well, God, I didn't trip and nothing negative happened, so I am taking this as your direction for me to do this.*

I started lessons that very week. By the end of January, my instructor decided I'd improved enough to pass me on to one of his teachers who taught more advanced students. Peter was from the Czech Republic, which had been carved from the old Czechoslovakia, the other half now Slovakia. Peter and I spend countless hours together over the following years as I was now taking three one-hour lessons a week. I'd always been naturally athletic, and I worked hard, so I was advancing rapidly.

Still, it was a surprise when Peter told me, "Eleanor, you're very good and learn quickly. I'd like to enter you with me in a dance competition this June."

I agreed, though with my lack of experience I was anxious I might let Peter down. We'd be dancing in front of a panel of ten judges and would have to perform two dances in each of the five styles featured—waltz, tango, fox trot, quick-step, and the Viennese waltz. This meant a total of ten dances. Competitors came from all over the continent, filling a nearby Sheraton that was hosting the competition. Dancers were divided into levels by experience and skill—bronze, silver, and gold, each of these divided into levels 1-3. Since I was a beginner, I would start in bronze, level one.

Upstairs, as I stepped into my rented ballroom dress, I prayed once again, *Okay, God, this is the last time I'm going to ask if this is really your will for me. If I do okay in this competition, I am going to take it once and for all that you've called me to this and that I should just pull out all the stops and enter this world of competitive dancing full force. And, please, I don't want this just to be about me. Show me how I can be a testimony to you out there, even if it is just dancing.*

I headed down to the dance floor determined just to enjoy the experience. There were video cameras everywhere as well as a professional photographer who did nothing but walk around taking pictures of the competition. Introducing myself to him, I said cheerfully, "Look, I've never done this before, and this will likely be my one and only competition. I might not have another chance to get professional photos of me dancing in costume, so would you mind taking plenty of my dances?"

There were ten other couples in my level. As the music started, I broke into a sweat, concentrating all my effort not to step on Peter's toes as we danced. It was a great surprise when the judges announced that I'd come in first place. Nor did it stop there. By the end of the competition, I'd won first place for all ten dances. As I stood up front, clutching all my medallions, the photographer approached me.

"I took as many pictures of you as I could from every angle," he told me. "You were really good! Are you sure you've never competed before?"

"No, I haven't," I assured him emphatically. "In fact, the first time I was ever on a dance floor was just six months ago."

"My goodness, I'd never have guessed!" he exclaimed. "You have such a presence when you dance. A special glow about you."

"I'd give any credit for that to God," I responded with a wide smile. "I'm a born-again Christian. God is who makes a difference in everything I do."

"That's it!" he exclaimed. "That's the glow I saw. By the way, I'm a born-again Christian too."

I suddenly realized that God had answered every one of my prayers. Not only had he given assurance this was where he'd called me, but he'd answered my prayer that I might give testimony to him as I danced. And just as I'd prayed when I was investigating what God's Word said about dancing, God had shown that I was not alone in this new endeavor. Going forward, I would encounter countless other brothers and sisters in Christ in the world of competitive ballroom dancing. I would also become a friend and American "mom" to many Eastern European young dancers in the competitive dance world.

Chapter Twenty-Six

Glorious Widowhood

Am I in the place of God? You intended to harm me, but God intended it for good to accomplish what is now being done, the saving of many lives. So then, don't be afraid.

—Genesis 50:19-21a

B allroom dancing has been part of my life ever since, and with it I can say that my "glorious widowhood" has reached fulfillment. Over the following years, I continued training and dancing with Peter, gradually moving up the competitive levels. To this point, I've won over one hundred first-place medallions in competition. I continued mentoring, counseling, speaking, and teaching Bible studies as well.

But a new burden had become part of my life. Shortly after my stepfather passed away, Mom had moved into assisted living. I'd invited her to live with me as Mom Isaacson had done, but she made clear she preferred being independent. Still, I visited her each day, acted as her chauffeur to appointments and shopping, took her with me to luncheons and other activities. She'd softened in her attitude towards me over the years, but she could still be very petulant and self-absorbed. But as I'd been my dear mother-in-law's caretaker too in her final years, so I determined I would to be to my birth mother, no matter how difficult this might prove.

Now that I was alone in the home Bob and I had built together, I'd also come to realize the house was too big for one person. Dear friends had recently moved to Willow Valley, a senior living community just south of Lancaster, PA, in the heart of Amish country. Whenever they returned to New Jersey for a visit, they'd ask me, "Why are you still rattling around this huge house? You should move out with us."

I resisted in part because I didn't consider myself a "senior". The last thing I wanted was to move to a retirement center where people just sat around waiting for life to end. But when I eventually visited, I discovered a beautiful community with spacious villas, townhouses, and condos spread out across 210 acres. Its residents were vibrant and active, and there were countless opportunities for community service as well as every possible amenity for quality of life.

But like every decision in my life, there was only one opinion that mattered. Walking around Willow Valley's beautiful vistas and landscaped gardens, I prayed, *Dear God, I can make a beautiful home here in Willow Valley. But Mom is content where she is. I can't move and leave her behind. So if this is your will, please make her want to come with me. If she doesn't, I'll know it isn't your will for me to move.*

Pulling out my cellphone right then and there, I called my mother. "Mom, guess where I am right now?" I explained what I was doing. "How would you like to move to Pennsylvania with me?"

Mom barely hesitated. "When do I pack?"

"Start now."

God had given me a clear answer. In March, 2002, I listed my New Jersey house for sale. This was just six months after the 9/11 Twin Towers attack, so that tragedy was fresh in all our minds. I moved Mom first to an assisted living facility that was part of the Willow Valley community. I purchased a beautiful villa in Willow Valley, smaller than the New Jersey house, but ample for one person.

I prayed that God would send just the right buyer for the New Jersey house, since I didn't want the home Bob and I had designed together to go to just anyone. In mid-July, I was hosting an open house for realtors when one woman walked in, dressed all in black and looking quite bedraggled. She looked like the most unlikely realtor to sell a high-value property like mine. But after looking around, she approached me.

"Your home is so beautiful. You know, I have friends who live not far from here. Two sisters. They aren't even looking to buy at the moment. But I know this house is exactly what they've always wanted. Would you mind if I bring them over this evening? I just want them to see it."

"Sure, why not!" I answered, not really expecting to see her again. The open house ended, and it was late enough I was already in my nightgown when the doorbell rang. I opened the door to see the realtor standing there, still in her bedraggled, black outfit.

Two other women were with her. They stepped into the entryway and immediately began exclaiming in delight. They walked down into the sunken living-room to look up at the cathedral ceiling and overlooking balcony. Once they'd seen the whole house and garden, the sisters told me, "We weren't even shopping for a house, but his is exactly the home we've always wanted. We'd like to buy it. Tonight, in fact."

My response wasn't as ecstatic. I held up my hand. "Now just hold it! I won't sell to just anyone. You need to understand this is a very special house. My husband and I designed every inch of it together. For years, this house has hosted Bible studies, prayer groups, and been a place where many people have seen their lives changed. So I want the next person who lives here to be someone who will love and appreciate it as I do."

The two sisters looked at each other, then at me. "Are you a born-again Christian?"

"I sure am," I answered.

They looked at each other again. "So are we. And we definitely want this house even more now."

By the end of the evening, the sisters had made an offer on the house and I had accepted. The next morning, the realtor stopped by with the check and final papers to sign. As I initialed each page, she said, "Eleanor, I can't tell you what selling this house means to me. Just to let you know, this is my first time back at work in almost a year."

"Oh, really, why is that?" I asked.

"Well, my son was on the ninety-third floor in the Twin Towers on 9/11. He didn't make it out. My husband and I haven't been able to stop grieving. Yesterday, they finally confirmed the identification of his DNA among the remains."

I realized now why she'd been dressed in black and looking so bedraggled. She went on, "Selling your house was such an encouraging event on a very terrible day."

I in turn had absolute peace God had arranged this entire sale. In October, 2002, I finally moved to Willow Valley. I'd brought no furnishings with me, so I became my own interior decorator. There was new furniture from Italy, classic tasseled drapes in red and gold, a kitchen trimmed in forest-green and white with white wicker furniture.

It turned out so beautiful that Willow Valley featured it in their 50,000-circulation magazine with one of my dance photos on the cover. That opened the door to do some modeling for Willow Valley advertising campaigns. I began entertaining as I'd done in New Jersey, including hosting a concert by the Millersville University chorus and fundraisers for the mayor's reelection campaign and Lancaster Symphony Orchestra. I found a new church home and a dance studio where I could continue training.

I also added one other change to my life. Clear back to my young adulthood, when I was living in deaf solitude, shy, stuttering, and dowdy, I'd had a secret longing I'd never shared with anyone. Oh, how I'd enjoyed the rare occasions when Dolores invited me for a drive in her convertible, top down, the breeze caressing my face and filling my nostrils with nature's rich scent. I'd dreamed of a convertible of my own. Not just any convertible. A bright-red convertible. Even when I'd finally been able to afford one, it had always seemed a little—well, unnecessary, worldly, a waste of money, all the adjectives Marian had drummed into my subconscious.

But as with my dancing, I've come to recognize that our heavenly Father judges less harshly than many who claim to follow him. Nor does he frown on his children enjoying his abundant blessings. The day I found myself in possession of a gorgeous, cherry-red BMW convertible, I felt eighteen-years-old again with my entire life stretching in front of me. I designed a personalized license plate that reads AT LAST 5, in recognition that this was the fulfillment of a five-decade dream.

I am still driving that convertible all over Lancaster County, and I still feel more youthful and alive every time I slide behind the wheel than I ever did in childhood, when I aged sixty years overnight. Once again, God was restoring the years the locusts had eaten, including everything I'd ever missed in the drabness of my childhood and young adult life.

CHAPTER TWENTY-SEVEN

HEALED AT LAST!

The Lord will be your everlasting light, and the days
of your mourning shall be ended.

—Isaiah 60:20

By now, Lancaster County had become home, and I
became increasingly involved in my new community.
I signed up as a mentor to students at nearby
Millersville University. I also went back to school, taking
courses at Lancaster Bible College and studying for
certification in counseling. I began teaching a children's
Bible club at a local elementary school as well as women's
Bible studies.

One blessing as Bob's widow was inheriting funds to share
with others. This has included a chapel for Lancaster
General Hospital in memory of Robert B. Isaacson, the
Isaacson Dance Studio at Millersville University, building
projects and student scholarships at Lancaster Bible College,
among other projects. I found myself serving as well on
numerous committees and boards—Lancaster Bible College,
Lancaster General Hospital's cancer center, Lancaster

Symphony Orchestra, Women's Symphony Association, Rotary Club, Susquehanna Speakers Association.

I was also speaking more than ever, an average of three times a week. I became Vice-President of the Susquehanna Speakers Association and more than once was voted Susquehanna Speaker of the Year. Since my speaking was based on events that you, my dear reader, have now read about in this book, I had an entire collage of poster boards made up as visual aids. One featured photos from my childhood in Nazi Germany, another the destruction and rebuilding of Plauen. Also included were Nazi atrocities and the concentrations camps. There were also photos of my married life and dancing career.

In all this, I continued caring faithfully for my mother. Every day, even when I had speaking engagements, I'd bring her to my home for lunch, give her a bath and massage, then put her down for a nap. While she rarely expressed appreciation, she enjoyed the attention and made her displeasure known if my schedule forced me to miss a day. Unlike Mom Isaacson, she'd steadfastly refused to attend any of my speaking engagements.

One day, I put her down for a nap before retrieving my poster boards from the car, where I'd stored them after a speaking engagement the day before. I had them set up on a table, checking each to make sure they were in good condition, when Mom emerged from her nap.

"Did you have a good nap, Mom?" I asked. Then on impulse, I added, "Hey, I have these pictures out from yesterday's speaking engagement. Would you like to take a look before I put them away?"

My only thought was that she might be interested in seeing the city where she'd grown up, both after the destruction and how it now looked rebuilt. But Mom didn't even glance at the poster boards before answering with flat disgust, "OMG, don't you get it? I don't care about any of that! I'm not in the least bit interested, and I don't want to ever see those pictures out again!"

Dear reader, I can tell you that as her words sunk in, I froze, inside and out. I was not only surprised, but deeply hurt. I had lived through all the terrible experiences displayed on those poster boards because the woman who'd given me birth abandoned me there. For the past sixty years, I'd been courteously and patiently listening to her complain about her hard life, unfair employers, jobs that were beneath her, unsatisfactory spouses, not to mention all the ways I fell short as a daughter. In all that time, she'd shown no interest in my past. But never before had she stated unequivocally she just didn't care what I'd gone through.

At that moment, my entire loveless childhood rose up in front of me like a full-color collage. The loneliness and rejection. The war and Nazi teachers. The bombs and hunger and constant fear. Coming on my own to America at age thirteen, only to face renewed rejection and loneliness. Not to mention, the death of my best friend and love of my life.

I wasn't prepared to confront the situation. But I was very quiet as I drove Mom back to her assisted living residence. Returning home, I picked up my Bible. How many times had I counseled others on how to handle injustice and unkindness? Keep forgiving. Keep praying. Keep on reading your Bible.

But this time I felt like David facing Goliath. But unlike David, Goliath seemed too big and powerful for me to defeat. I began to pray. *Dear God, I thought I'd finally put my childhood and all that happened there in the past. That I'd forgiven my parents and moved on. How many more years and how many more painful encounters with Mom will it take before I find complete healing?*

As I sat there, I faced the truth. I would not be able to put the past behind me and find healing until I confronted my mother. But I had no idea how, and I was scared to death even contemplating it. Here I was, a strong, confident adult woman, while Mom was a frail, dependent nonagenarian. And yet she still had such power to hurt me that I felt helpless at the thought of facing her.

Besides, if I did confront her, I knew how she'd react. She'd brush it off with a laugh and her usual delusions. Hitler had never really existed. Or at least he hadn't been such an evil tyrant as people claimed. There'd been no war. Or if there'd been a real conflict, the whole thing had been grossly exaggerated, and her daughter certainly hadn't suffered any hardships in it.

Okay, God, I can't do this! I admitted. *You'll have to help me confront her. And it has to be in such a way she can't just walk off. So if you want me to do this, please give me just the right opportunity. The ball is in your court now!*

Maybe that seems a little too familiar in talking to God. But when God is your heavenly Father and closest friend in heaven and on earth, he doesn't mind you talking to him as bluntly as you feel. Just read in the Bible how Jeremiah, Habakkuk, Jonah, and other prophets talked to God when they were upset. And how kindly and lovingly their Creator responded.

I've said before, dear reader, that when you pray, you'd better be prepared for God's answer. Just one week later, I picked up my mother, planning to take her out somewhere for lunch. We'd paused at a red light when she looked over at me. "By the way, the next time I come to your house, you show me some nice pictures of my family, not of the war."

With a uniquely German dismissive hand gesture, she added, "I'm not interested in any of that. I just don't care!"

That was my breaking point. Pulling over to the side of the road, I turned off the engine and locked the car doors so she couldn't get out. If you think Fourth of July has fireworks, you should have been in my back seat right then. I was so upset that I shook all over as sixty years of pent-up pain boiled out.

"Mom, how can you say that? How can you say you don't care and you're not interested when the daughter you just dropped off over there had to go through all that death and pain and bombings and invasion and hunger? Not to mention, not having a mother or a father like all the other children in school. How dare you say you don't care and aren't interested! What kind of mother are you? You are a terrible woman and a terrible human being. I've never treated my worst enemy as badly as you've treated me all these years, denying all the pain I went through because of you.

Taking a deep breath, I went on, "But you can be thankful I'm a Christian and that I have God in my life, who loves me even if you don't. He has used all these horrible things to shape me into a loving, giving, forgiving compassionate, glorious woman. I want you to know I will never be like you in any way, and I am proud of that. I have made it my life commitment to be a better woman than you have been and to have a positive impact on the people in my life as you never have. And everything you took from me, God has restored by giving me a better marriage, a better husband, a bigger house, and a more accomplished, fulfilling life. And God did it all in front of you so that you had to watch!"

Okay, maybe that wasn't all so diplomatic. But I meant every word. Just speaking them was such a release of all my pent-up emotions that I could feel their weight falling off my shoulders like Christian's burden in Pilgrim's Progress. The twenty-third psalm, often called the Shepherd's Psalm, since it compares God's watch-care over his children to a good shepherd caring for his flock, says of our heavenly Shepherd:

> You prepare a table before me in the presence of my
> enemies.

> —Psalm 23:5

One interpretation of this image is God heaping his abundant blessings on his children in full view of those who have hurt and wronged them. Similarly, when Jesus spoke to the persecuted church of Philadelphia, he said of their enemies:

> I will make them come and fall down at your feet
> and acknowledge that I have loved you.

> —Revelations 3:9

Dear reader, as I told Mom that day in no uncertain terms, God has indeed richly blessed me and made evident his immeasurable love for me in the presence of my enemies, of whom my own birth mother and father were not least. And God will do the same for you. Perhaps right now you feel surrounded and overwhelmed by those who've wronged you and abused you. You feel locked away in a dark dungeon of injustice and unkindness from which you see no escape.

But if you don't possess the key to unlock the dungeon door, God does. You may need to sit patiently for a while. God may be permitting temporary darkness and captivity to teach you vital lessons about kindness, compassion, empathy for others. The first important thing to learn is to stop seeing your dark place as a prison, but as a spiritual sanctuary, as I came to understand that dark bedroom into which my aunt locked me.

Secondly, you need to recognize that God loves you and that he won't abandon you in the darkness. Jesus says, "I am the way, the truth, and the life (John 14:6). If you haven't yet placed your faith in Jesus as your personal Savior, you need to do so. As you learn to trust him, he will transform your dungeon of despair into a spiritual sanctuary. And in his perfect timing, God will unlock the door, his light will flood in, and you will step out into freedom.

I was experiencing just such a release from my prison of buried emotions as God gave me the words to confront my mother. During all this, Mom just sat there, her head turned away from me, staring out the side passenger window. I kept expecting her to tell me to shut up. But she didn't say a single word. I think she recognized just how angry I was and for once was afraid of my response if she told me to be quiet.

At last, I finished my say. I hadn't realized what a very heavy burden I'd been carrying all these years until I'd gotten it off my chest. For the first time in my life, I felt completely healed of all my emotional pain. I sat there with my head bowed. There was a long silence, Mom still staring out the window to her right.

Finally, I started the engine and shifted the car into gear. Slowly, I moved out onto the road. One minute passed. Then another. Eventually, Mom turned around to face the front windshield.

"So where are we going for lunch?" she asked cheerfully.

That was all she said. Never then or in the future did Mom make mention of what I'd said to her. I drove to her favorite Chinese restaurant, feeling as exhausted as though I'd just survived five years of guerrilla warfare. We were sipping egg-drop soup when Mom looked up at me with a smile. "You know, Eleanor, you are such a good person. And so smart. You can do everything so good, I tell people."

"Thank you," I responded. "How is your egg-drop soup?"

Now I felt like David after he landed that stone on Goliath's forehead. After all these years, God had finally given me the courage to do what needed to be done, and I have a feeling there were angels cheering at that moment up in heaven.

From that day on, Mom behaved towards me like a perfect angel. She'd always had a gift for denial and playing a role, turning charm on and off at will. And after my outburst, I think she was scared I might in turn abandon her if she wasn't careful how she treated me. Whatever the reason, I was just happy to finally have the mother I'd always wanted. She'd hug me and kiss me, and she couldn't compliment me enough to others. "My Eleanor is such a good driver. She is so good to me. Have you seen her dance? So beautiful! And so smart!"

Mom lived to a hundred years and six months old. During those final years, I became the mother she herself had never had. She died a very happy, nurtured, and loved woman, and we became very close. She too came to know Christ before she died.

Her mind remained clear and sharp to the end, but during that last year, if I arrived later than usual, she'd beg me anxiously, "Oh, don't leave me, Eleanor! I thought you were going to leave me!"

I always assured her that I loved her, forgave her, and would never leave her. I was reminded of the biblical patriarch Joseph, who had also endured rejection by his own family, abuse, injustice, captivity, and so much more (Genesis 37-50). But through those very hardships, he eventually reached a pinnacle of fame and fortune, and God used him to save millions from famine, including his own brothers, who had betrayed him. When at the end of Joseph's life story, his brothers beg his forgiveness for their betrayal, Joseph responds:

> Don't be afraid. Am I in the place of God? You intended to harm me, but God intended it for good to accomplish what is now being done, the saving of many lives.
>
> —Genesis 50:19-20

And that is how I've come to feel about my mother. I can now see that she was God's instrument in chiseling me and refining me. In his wisdom and infinite love, God knew precisely what kind of mother and life experience I needed to become the woman he'd designed me to be. A woman able to love. To forgive. To empathize with the pain of others and to show compassion to both the hurting and those who have inflicted hurt. To mentor and counsel those going through abuse, abandonment, crisis, loneliness. To offer others the same comfort I have been granted.

I've never had children of my own, but God has made me a mother to so many who are motherless as well as to my own mother in her last years. I was once friendless and alone, but God has made me a friend to many who were friendless. My home is constantly filled with young people and old to whom I've been privileged to show God's love. Whatever ungodly, unloving, and unjust people in my past may have meant for evil, God has transformed into good.

And in the end, I can say with Joseph that it's all been worth it!

Epilogue

Surrendering the Baton

Let us run with endurance the race that is set before
us, looking unto Jesus, the author and finisher of
our faith.

—Hebrews 12:1b-2

So I come to the end of this book, if not my story.
There is so much more I could say. Other tales and
God-lessons I could share. With my continued good
health and a mother who lived beyond her century mark, I
anticipate plenty more life adventures with my Lord and
Savior, if he so chooses. But only so much will fit into one
book. Maybe one day I'll write a sequel.

But let me finish by going back to the beginning. When we
started this journey, I shared the analogy of a puzzle box and
how the days and years and events of our lives are like the
pieces of a puzzle. Some dark. Some light. All kinds of
shapes. Heaped together, they are a chaotic jumble with no
seeming purpose at all. But when they are pieced together,
the beautiful picture they form becomes clear.

So it is with our lives. Good and bad. Sad and happy. Few or many. If we can't see any pattern or purpose in the days that make up the puzzle pieces of our lives, God does. He knew what every one of those days would hold before our bodies were ever knit together in our mother's womb (Psalm 139:13-16). And when the last puzzle piece is fit into place, we will see and understand the beautiful picture God is creating of our lives.

But there's another analogy I'd like to end with. One that rises often to my mind because Bob and I spent so many delightful hours together at Carnegie Hall, the Lincoln Center, and other concert venues. It is that of a well-tuned symphony orchestra. If you come in early before a concert starts and sit listening to the performers tuning their instruments, you'd think them capable of only the most awful cacophony. The piccolo's shrillness is drowning out the oboe and flute. The violins and cellos all sound like a bunch of cats when a rocking chair pinches their tails. The drums are as clamorous as New York City traffic.

And just as a puzzle has dark pieces and light, so these instruments are emitting minor, mournful chords, brightly cheerful ones, others that are loud and discordant. Mixed all together, it doesn't sound like music, but pure chaos.

Then the orchestra conductor steps onto his podium. He raises his baton. Every instrument falls silent. Every musician fixes their eyes on the conductor. Then with a down-stroke of the baton, woodwinds, strings, brass, and percussion raise their voices in perfect harmony. Minor, major, and even the occasional discordant chords combine to form a melodic line. So long as the performers keep their eyes on the conductor and follow every direction of his baton, the result is a beautiful symphony to delight their audience.

Our lives are like that too, a messy chaotic cacophony of notes and pitches with no rhyme or reason, meaning or purpose, unless a conductor steps in with a baton to bring order to the mess. At least that was my past life. And because I thought it was my responsibility to sort out the chaos, I had the baton clutched tightly in my hand, thinking if I could just wave it around long enough, I might be able to turn my mess into music.

Of course, that proved far beyond my capability. Thankfully, we too have a conductor, Jesus Christ, the Author and Finisher of our faith (Hebrews 12:2). Author and Finisher means Jesus doesn't just initiate our walk of faith, but he will continue to work in us, transforming the cacophony of our lives into a sweet-sounding, harmonious symphony. A work that will not be finished until we join him in glory:

> Being confident of this, that he who began a good work in you will carry it on to completion until the day of Christ Jesus.
>
> —Philippians 1:6

But I've already mentioned that God is a gentleman. If we want Jesus to turn our chaos into music, we must be willing to let go of our baton and hand it over to him. And even that isn't enough. We must keep our eyes on him as we run the race of this life, so we can respond to every baton wave of our heavenly Conductor.

What is the result? Well, let's consider what a conductor does with that baton. He unifies the performers into a common purpose. He sets the tempo. He controls and shapes the interpretation and pacing of the music. He executes clear directives necessary to turn individual sounds and beats into recognizable lines of music.

So too, when we surrender the baton of our lives to Jesus, he brings us into the unity of God's family. The tempo and rhythm of our daily activities become his to direct. And if we follow his clear instructions given in his Word to protect and guide us, the chaos of our lives will become beautiful music.

On Thursday, Feb. 25th, 1954, at 8:45 in the morning, I gladly handed the baton of my life to Jesus Christ, my Lord and Savior. He turned the mess of my past—the loneliness, rejection, pain, fear, hunger, grief—into music. Today, sixty-three years later, I can testify with great joy that the music is still playing.

Now what about you?

Eleanor Isaacson

Born in New Jersey, speaker, author, and WWII survivor Eleanor Isaacson was raised till age thirteen in East Germany. Returning to the USA with neither English nor family, she overcame every obstacle to graduate with a double Bachelor's Degree magna cum laude, become a successful business entrepreneur, and marry renowned scientist Dr. Robert Isaacson. She is also a competitive ballroom dancer with more than 100 first-place wins.

Jeanette Windle

Award-winning author and investigative journalist Jeanette Windle has lived in six countries and traveled in thirty-plus. She has written twenty fiction and non-fiction books and mentors writers on five continents.

Letters to Eleanor!

These letters were sent to Eleanor soon after her book was released. Some are friends, and some are well-wishers who were overwhelmed by her narrative.

❋

Dear Eleanor,

After three days of looking at the cover and praying, I opened the book and started reading your story. Once I started reading it was very difficult for me to put it down... Your story telling was so vivid and riveting. I could hear the bomber coming and I wanted to hold your hand while running for protection; I felt your hunger as well. I wanted to embrace your aunt for locking you in the room; I sense that she was doing this for your protecting from the beginning. I was relieved to know that my instincts were correct, as you explain later in your story.

As I consider reading I could not believe how indestructible you are. Your roller coaster life of great awards (sharing your love of God with others, getting married to the love of your life, winning awards for dancing...) and not so great events (living through the holocaust, returning home to unloving family, losing your loving husband, losing your hearing...) you did not reak or become discouraged in your faith in God. Your dedication to God increased with each event good or bad, even before you knew who God is. This would not be true for so many of us, especially me. I enjoy the bible quotes throughout the book. You have encouraged me to pick up my bible and start reading again.

Your book was a wonderful gift. Thank you so much. I pray that God continues to watch over you, protect you, and love you.

—*Carmen*

❋

Dear Eleanor,

Your book is inspired, it's brilliant, it's unforgettable, it's beautifully written… it's every bit the tribute to your Bob and to you and to your invisible God that it should be…

Last night I had some quiet time to start it and I thought I would read a few chapters. Well! I could not put it down. I can't wait to lose myself again in your life and your love and your hope and your inspiration.

Your book is one of the best books I have ever read. Actually I can't think of a better book. It's an emotional read, and FILLED with hope and love. The Bible verses are so cleverly interwoven and appropriate. The verses have come to life for me.

Eleanor, I can't say enough. Thank you, with every ounce of gratitude in me, for writing this book.

—*Sally*

✺

Dear Eleanor,

Thank you so much for sharing your most inspirational book. It is a true treasure. I will pass it to other friends.

Fondly,

Cheryl

✺

Your book has been a wonderful testimony to God's faithfulness in every aspect of your life.

—*Dolores*

✺

Eleanor,

I finished reading your book in a few days and I enjoyed every minute of it! You have a beautiful story and the book is well-written and filled with truth and hope. And the perfect bonus is that I have the privilege of knowing the author personally. ☺ Congratulations on your accomplishment!

Love,

Janelle

※

Dearest Eleanor,

I just wanted to thank you for putting your story in words. <u>LOVED YOUR BOOK</u>!!

I'm just sorry your story had to end.

I am <u>truly amazed</u> at how you clung to God again and again… How you became a woman of love and generosity despite all you went through as a child… Your story has encouraged me to press on, trusting in the Lord who gave His life for me. My husband and I signed up for a free ballroom dance lesson this Saturday. You inspired me!

—Colleen

※

Dear Eleanor,

I read the first two chapters immediately… I was in tears as I read your book – it was so special, so personal, and a testimony to the glorious working of God.

—Diane

※

Dear Eleanor,

Thank you so much for putting your life story into print. We have both read it and are now going to pass it on to a friend.

Your expressions were unbelievable. You have been through so much and survived so much. ..I loved the spiritual part of the book. It was laid out so clearly. Thank you Eleanor for a wonderful read.

—Caryl and George

✻

Eleanor, I have just finished reading your life story in *"Dancing from Darkness."* It is an exciting and encouraging account of how God guided and protected your life, even before you knew His name. Your life is an inspiration filled with many life lessons for each of us as you let God be your Father and Shepherd. Thank you for including so much scripture to point us to the truths you were discovering in your life. I am privileged to know you.

—Josie

✻

Dear Eleanor,

What an inspiration you are to all of us around you, Eleanor!!! Jeremiah 29:11: *For I know the plans I have for you*, Eleanor, says the Lord…

—Carol

✻

Dear Eleanor,

Who knows how many lives will be changed?

—Barbara

＊

Dear Eleanor,

We read your whole book within two days of receiving it. It is a tremendous witness of what the Lord can do for a person totally willing to serve Him.

Thank you for sharing your life with us in the form of this autobiography you wrote and gave to us. We both have devoured the whole book. And we are thankful to our common Savior for keeping you safe every moment of your life, so that you could share with us and the world all that He has done for you to keep you alive. You are not only alive, but abundantly blessed through all your trials, so that you could be doubly blessed in the special favors He has given you throughout your life as well.

—*Tom and Claire*

＊

Dear Eleanor,

So I just completed your book. It was so enthralling even though I could only read so many chapters at a time because of being on vacation and distractions.

I finished with a host of emotions relating to my own life and yet so inspired by your life, faith, and desire to be better. I will have this your story dwell with me for weeks, months, and years to come. On a much smaller scale I relate so well with your story as my story growing up feels so similar in hurts, pain, loneliness and eventually faith and trusting in my Lord and Savior.

—*Carol*

＊

Dear Eleanor,

Your book is fantastic, inspiring, and no doubt took an enormous amount of time and organization to make this book happen with such inspiration. The book cover is eye-catching, inviting and well designed with a very beautiful and blessed lady all dressed for the most glorious ballroom dance with God who dwells in her devoted heart... WOW!

God surely has a glorious plan for you – it began from day one. You are living a powerful guided life of extreme challenges, faithfulness, sadness, and extreme joyous times... all for His glory. Your book has shared much of your life, mastered the temptations of free will, and with grace, have graciously overcome temptation with the Lord leading the way. I love how the book always points to scripture with relevant Bible verses made this read inspirational. You have truly given the Holy Spirit a permanent full-time 24/7 job of guiding your life – BRAVO!

...I have shared your book with many... one told me she is taking your book to her book club. I have also recommended your book to my friends and family here and in France. Eleanor, I know your book has inspired me and pray it will do the same for many others.

ISAIAH 49:16: *I have written your name on my hand.* Eleanor, this is you in large bold letters!

With love and prayer and gratitude and faith,

Debbie

❋

Dear Eleanor,

We are reading your scintillating life story, and it is a winner!

—*Ginny and Jim*

✻

Dear Eleanor,

What a blessing this book will be to thousands! I am halfway through and have already been so blessed! Not only is it well written, but it uplifts Jesus Christ. God has and continues to use your life-story to change the lives of others for Him.

—*Ruth*

✻

Dear Eleanor,

Once I received your book from my friend Sally in the mail, I read the first couple of chapters and then could not stop reading it!!! I finished the whole book the next day.

I love your book. It was so edifying the way you exalted the Lord throughout your trying and abused life. Having run a counseling center for many years that dealt with the abused and broken, your words of being proactive and not giving up and always trusting in the Lord's presence in each circumstance was a delight, and challenge, to my soul. Your life legacy is important to share and will touch millions as people resonate with your struggles and miracle leadings. You have honored the Lord by always having the heart to share your faith with others and not be reticent to give word of your deep faith. May peace and grace be multiplied unto you, Eleanor.

Most sincerely,

—*Barbara*

✻

Dear Eleanor,

We found your story CAPTIVATING!!

—*Jack and Carolyn*

✳

Dear Eleanor,

I am so glad you wrote your wonderful story – it tells so much of your exciting journey, with GOD, then your earthly life. Thank you for writing it, thank you for sharing it with us all, dear Eleanor. And there's more to come, coming up!

You are Great! You know…

I'll be reading your book again, later. Right now, my sister borrowed it.

—*Jessie*

Made in the USA
Lexington, KY
16 May 2018